# the *ultimate* APPLIQUÉ GUIDEBOOK

 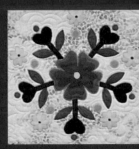 

150 Patterns,
Hand & Machine Techniques, History,
Step-by-Step Instructions,
Keys to Design & Inspiration

## Annie Smith

Text and Artwork copyright © 2010 by Annie Smith

Photography copyright © 2010 by C&T Publishing, Inc.

Publisher: Amy Marson

Creative Director: Gailen Runge

Acquisitions Editor: Susanne Woods

Editor: Deb Rowden

Technical Editor: Teresa Stroin and Janice Wray

Copyeditor/Proofreader: Wordfirm Inc.

Cover/Book Designer: Kristen Yenche

Production Coordinator: Jenny Leicester

Production Editor: Alice Mace Nakanishi

Illustrator: Guy Smith

Photography by Christina Carty-Francis and Diane Pedersen of C&T Publishing, Inc., unless otherwise noted

Published by C&T Publishing, Inc., P.O. Box 1456, Lafayette, CA 94549

Library of Congress Cataloging-in-Publication Data

Smith, Annie, (Annie Williamson)

 The ultimate appliqué guidebook : 150 patterns, hand & machine techniques, history, step-by-step instructions, keys to design & inspiration / by Annie Smith.

   p. cm.

Includes bibliographical references and index.

ISBN 978-1-60705-005-6 (softcover)

1. Appliqué. 2. Quilting. I. Title.

TT779.S62 2010

746.44'5--dc22

                    2010007572

Printed in China

10  9  8  7  6  5  4  3  2  1

# Dedication

This book is lovingly dedicated to my husband, Guy.

Your help and support have been unlimited since I started this crazy "hobby" during the first year of our marriage. As quilting became my career and crept into our family life, I always said that I couldn't do this without you—and it has never been more true than with the writing and compilation of this book. This is just as much your book as it is mine.

Thank you for being, and remaining through these 30 years, my best friend!

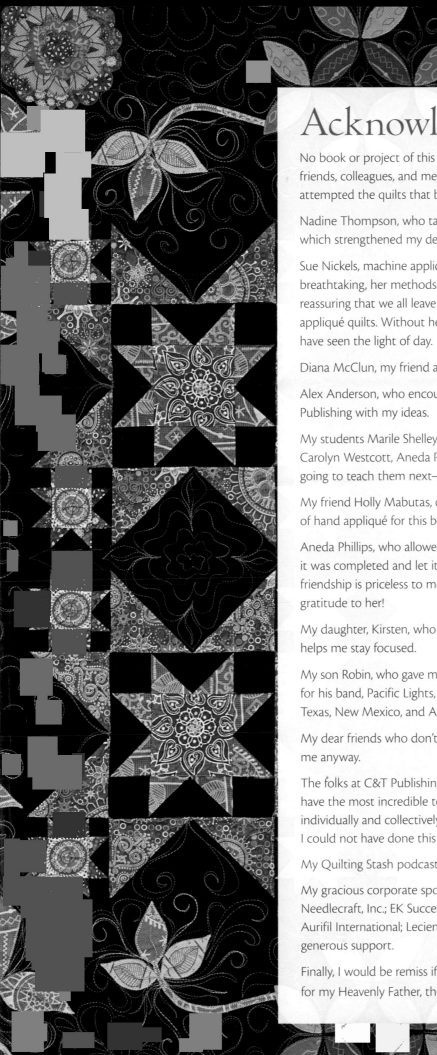

# Acknowledgments

No book or project of this scope is ever completed without help from valued friends, colleagues, and mentors. I could never have written this book, nor attempted the quilts that began this journey, without the help of the following:

Nadine Thompson, who taught me a beautifully simple way to hand appliqué, which strengthened my desire to make an appliqué quilt.

Sue Nickels, machine appliqué quilter and teacher extraordinaire. Sue's work is breathtaking, her methods are compelling, and her teaching style is so warm and reassuring that we all leave her classroom fully confident that we can make beautiful appliqué quilts. Without her expertise and encouragement, this book would never have seen the light of day.

Diana McClun, my friend and mentor, who offered encouragement and wisdom.

Alex Anderson, who encouraged me to write a book and to approach C&T Publishing with my ideas.

My students Marile Shelley, Joanna Johnson, Sue Kobata, Lesa Santos, Joyce Mukuno, Carolyn Westcott, Aneda Phillips, and Missy Fox, who wanted to learn what I was going to teach them next—and that became my *West of Baltimore* quilt.

My friend Holly Mabutas, of Eat Cake Graphics, who generously shared her method of hand appliqué for this book.

Aneda Phillips, who allowed me to borrow her *West of Baltimore* quilt as soon as it was completed and let it travel all over the United States for two years. Her friendship is priceless to me, and I cannot adequately express my heartfelt gratitude to her!

My daughter, Kirsten, who always has an eye for just the right placement—and helps me stay focused.

My son Robin, who gave me the opportunity to work on the book while chaperoning for his band, Pacific Lights, while on tour through Colorado, Kansas, Oklahoma, Texas, New Mexico, and Arizona.

My dear friends who don't hear from me as often as they would like and still like me anyway.

The folks at C&T Publishing, who took a chance on a new author and a new book. I have the most incredible team and have been richly blessed by their expertise. They individually and collectively worked with me to make this book the best it could be. I could not have done this without their enthusiasm, encouragement, and direction.

My Quilting Stash podcast friends, fans, and students.

My gracious corporate sponsors—Northcott Silk Inc.; Shades Textiles; Clover Needlecraft, Inc.; EK Success; Robert Kaufman Fabrics; Cherrywood Fabrics Inc.; Aurifil International; Lecien Corporation / Art and Hobby Division—who provided generous support.

Finally, I would be remiss if I did not acknowledge the incalculable gratitude I have for my Heavenly Father, the ultimate source of my talent and inspiration.

# TABLE OF

# CONTENTS

## Design Use

The appliqué shapes and motifs presented in this book can also be used and adapted for any other type of appliqué: crafts, wearables, home décor—anything you desire. It is a resource book for you.

These designs are not limited to use on quilts only. Use any of the designs in this book to embellish a sweatshirt, jacket, or other article of clothing; a board book; in scrapbooking and cardmaking; or in any other craft that could include appliqué.

If you use the designs for any item that will appear in a competition or as a photo in print, you are required to credit the author and book title as your inspiration or source.

# Introduction

I remember when I was first struck by the beauty of appliqué quilts. It happened when I walked into my future sister-in-law's home and saw an appliquéd and embroidered quilt stretched on a quilting frame, with a cluster of ladies quilting around it. Having sewn garments in high school, I knew that after I had my first child, I would become a quilting mom—although making an appliqué quilt was on a far distant horizon. My first quilt for my first child, a daughter, materialized two years later in the form of a hand-pieced sampler. It is sweet but far from perfect.

My first foray into appliqué was a quilt featuring a little red schoolhouse and hearts. I staystitched ¼" around each of the shapes and pressed the edges under—just like I would have sewn a garment. Obviously, I didn't know anything about appliqué! Then I tried the crafty way to do appliqué, by satin stitching on rip-stop nylon to make a flag for girls' camp—with disastrous results. That's when I learned the phrase that quilters use for imperfect projects: "If you can't see it on a galloping horse, it doesn't matter." This became my motto for the next decade.

I even tried to learn the needle-turn method of hand appliqué and just couldn't get the hang of it. Looking longingly at those beautiful appliqué quilts, I felt intimidated by them until I took a class that freed me from the fear of creating an appliqué quilt of my own.

In 1999, I chose Sue Nickels's weeklong workshop at my first Empty Spools Seminar. I was attracted by Sue's sample for the class, *The Beatles Quilt.* Sue showed us slides of the award-winning quilt made with her sister, Pat Holly.

 **Note** At the quilt's first showing, Sue Nickels's and Pat Holly's *The Beatles Quilt* won "Best of Show" at the American Quilter's Society show in Paducah, Kentucky, in 1998. The quilt is on permanent display at the National Quilt Museum in Paducah.

Sitting in the darkened room, looking at appliqué images of Beatles songs and recalling memories associated with those songs—the soundtrack of my teenage life—was overwhelming, emotional, and inspiring. I fell in love with Sue's method of machine appliqué, adopted it as my preferred technique, and knew that I would make appliqué quilts for the rest of my life.

The idea for this book came to me while I was working on a special project. I was invited to design a small quilt and a full-length coat for Rachel Clark's special exhibit "Off the Bed, On the Back" for Pacific International Quilt Festival in 2008. Each quilter was assigned a quilt technique, such as Log Cabin style, Hawaiian appliqué, paper piecing, and so on. Mine was Baltimore Album–style appliqué—based on my *West of Baltimore* quilt. I decided to adapt some of those motifs for the small quilt and then carry over those designs to adorn the coat (page 67). While I was elbow-deep in the project, I realized that I was using only elements of my original designs. What a great idea it would be to create a book that would be a resource for other quilters looking for appliqué designs! While there have been many books written about ways to make appliqué quilts and offering whole block designs, there are no books that present appliqué *elements* from which you can pick and choose the types of flowers, leaves, birds, and so on that you would like to use for your own quilt. A sourcebook of individual appliqué designs—or elements—is, I feel deeply, needed and useful.

This book is the culmination of my work for the last 25 years, and with it I offer all my knowledge of and expertise in appliqué. I grant you permission—and encourage you—to play with the designs, create beautiful appliqué quilts, and have fun with this book. I hope that the projects and the quilts in the gallery will inspire you and that you will enjoy this, *The Ultimate Appliqué Guidebook.*

Here's to making beautiful appliqué!

*Happy Quilting!*

*Annie*

*Kirsten's Baby Quilt.* Here is my first baby quilt, a sampler pieced and quilted by hand in 1981. I made it using the fabrics available at the time, cotton/poly-blend solids and calicoes. About the navy fabric: I don't know why I used it, except that I thought I needed "just one more fabric"—a notion that I still subscribe to!

*Love for Learning*, Annie Smith, San Jose, California, 1984, 50″ × 50″

I originally made this quilt with yellow gingham sashing that was so loosely woven that the seams disintegrated within a year. I loved the quilt so much that I completely disassembled it, chose a new yellow calico, and remade the quilt. You can still see the ghost of the original quilting on the back of the quilt.

# How to Use This Book

This is a sourcebook of design elements. In Chapter 12: Catalog of Appliqué Design Elements (page 105), you will find a variety of flowers, leaves, birds, vases, and much more that will allow you to design your own layouts for blocks, borders, and quilts. Follow my patterns exactly, as in the projects in Chapter 9: Three Appliqué Projects to Get You Started (page 72), or mix and match and make changes as you are inspired.

There are pages of multisize flowers, so you can use the size you desire. Vase handles are provided separately so you can choose which handle you like best. Wings of insects can be modified, and the direction in which birds are flying or sitting can be reversed by flipping the pattern that you trace or by making a mirror-image copy on a printer. The patterns can also be reduced or enlarged on a photocopier.

Another option is to use my design elements in conjunction with an existing pattern from another book. My favorite appliqué books are listed in the bibliography (page 155).

I hope you will take the time to read the book from cover to cover, as this is much more than just a pattern or project book—it is also about inspiration. My aim is to inspire you to create your own appliqué quilts from these designs. You will find tips and special features to assist you along the way. To get you started, I present three projects in this book that vary in size (small, medium, and large) and complexity (from beginner to experienced).

We gave this book a special binding so you can lay it open flat to a pattern page and trace any of the designs using fusible web or freezer paper. Also for your convenience, each appliqué pattern is presented as a whole piece:

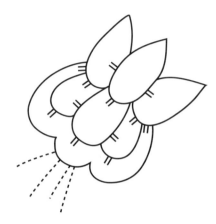

This is easier to work with than a pattern with sections for you to combine:

I hope you draw on the wealth of inspiration and appliqué designs in this book to create your own appliqué quilt!

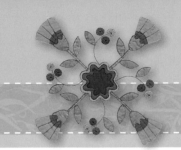

# CHAPTER 1

# What Is *Fine* Appliqué?

*A thing of beauty is a joy forever.* —John Keats

**Fine** *adj.*

1. in a good, acceptable, or comfortable condition (informal)

2. very thin, sharp, or delicate

3. very good to look at

4. far better than the average

5. showing special skill, detail, or intricacy, especially in artistic work

6. set very closely and carefully together

Excellent, delicate, refined—these are all exact definitions of the fine appliqué that I will share with you in this book.

When I began quilting in 1980, appliqué quilts were appliquéd by hand and hand quilted. The longarm quilting machine wouldn't make its appearance until 1994, and it would take several more years for machine appliqué and machine quilting to become an "acceptable" technique in quilt competitions.

Machine appliqué caught my eye in 1984, when I noticed beautiful craft projects offered in *Better Homes and Gardens* magazine.

## 1980s Machine Appliqué

The early '80s trend for everything country encouraged home décor colors such as mauve, French blue, peach, and seafoam green—and we had access to those color choices in our fabrics, too. We decorated our kitchens with French country geese ceramics and our walls with embroidery hoops of cross-stitched sayings on gingham. Machine appliqué sometimes adorned those hoops or wallhangings, and it was made with a thick satin stitch that was hard to stitch solidly and evenly. It was difficult to get the satin stitch perfect. My motifs lacked stabilizer and usually came out misshapen, with the stitching thicker than the fabrics.

## The Sweatshirt Generation

After the emergence of satin-stitch machine appliqué, clever crafters began putting appliqué images on the fronts of sweatshirts. We loved wearing unique sweatshirts, rather than ones with silk-screened logos. The designs were inspired by coloring-book images and embellished with buttons, embroidery floss, and puff paint. These unique sweatshirts were found most easily at home holiday boutiques, but eventually they were mass-produced by manufacturers.

## Baltimore Revival

Thanks to the Maven of Appliqué, Elly Sienkiewicz, 1994 marked the resurgence of Baltimore-style appliqué. It is this style of appliqué that I refer to as "fine." *Excellent, delicate, refined*—these words define the appliqué that is found in antique Baltimore Album–style quilts and the contemporary appliqué quilts that we meticulously make today. Baltimore Album quilts are the ones that grabbed me and held me spellbound. It was those quilts that inspired Sue Nickels and Pat Holly to create *The Beatles Quilt*, and thus inspired me to learn how to create the appliqué that is found within this book.

# Fine Appliqué

Fine appliqué, whether produced by hand or machine, is appliqué that is created thoughtfully, lovingly, and, I might say, with determination. Fine appliqué is detailed in design and carefully crafted. Observers may refer to it as "precise," "intricate," and "complex."

Fine appliqué generally includes very detailed piecing in its designs—such as Baltimore Album–style appliqué. It is not unusual to see elements as small as ¼" in diameter, with finer stitching than in other types of appliqué. Flowers can be layered or stacked. Vines and stems are typically made using bias strips. Animals and personal motifs are included, along with embroidered or hand-penned detailing.

Fine machine appliqué has the look and feel of hand appliqué. Contemporary sewing machines can mimic the stitch of hand appliqué very well. Machine appliqué techniques can re-create the softness of hand appliqué, as the fusible material is cut away on the inside of the shape before it is fused to the fabric. This technique allows only the edge to be fused in place and then edgestitched, leaving a soft appliqué piece with no fusible stiffness underneath.

Fine machine appliqué is made to last, as it is created with great precision and detail. The finished products are museum quality and competition worthy.

The current trend in quiltmaking, as I write this book, is focused on quick and easy designs, using large-print fabrics for large spaces and simple methods of construction. I made similar quilts when I began quilting in 1980. As my skills improved, I began to look for more challenging projects. When I made my first machine appliqué quilt, I could see the boundaries of regular quiltmaking fall by the wayside. Now I have the ability to make any design and apply it any way I wish. I can make a quilt that challenges me and improves my skills—on a project that may well become my masterpiece or close to it.

In summary, fine appliqué mirrors the exquisite work found in museums and the books that we examine with awe. We see these works and wish we could make something remotely close to representing those works of old … and so we can.

*Colonial Girls*, Florence Lily Woest Borrowman, Gridley, California, 1950, 74" × 80"

The Aunt Martha patterns inspired many a quilter. *Colonial Girls* is one of these patterns. The girl and border fabric pieces were hand appliquéd using a blanket stitch. The quilt was hand quilted and saved for special occasions. It was given to the quiltmaker's (Lily's) oldest granddaughter, Sharon Smith, as a wedding gift one year after Lily's death. Lily was best known for her quilts made from 1" squares and 2" squares. These she made for her daughters using scraps of fabric given to her by friends.

*Pickle Road Garden*, Annie Smith, San Jose, California, 2007, 54″ × 54″

I designed this quilt using Mark Lipinski's first fabric line, Katmandu, and Jeff Turner's art designs from the April/May 2007 issue of *Quilter's Home* magazine.

*Aunt Mimi's Flower Garden*, Elsie M. Campbell, Dodge City, Kansas, 2006, 83" × 83".
Machine appliqué, machine piecing, and machine quilting.

Inspired by a red, green, and cheddar traditional appliqué quilt that was a "Best of Show" winner at the Quilters' Heritage Celebration in Lancaster, Pennsylvania, one year, Elsie designed her own original appliqué blocks. The blocks were completed one or two at a time over the course of several years, but the circular block setting came to her in a dream early one morning while she was visiting her son in San Francisco. The border appliqué and Celtic knot designs were worked out as separate steps in the design process. This quilt was her first bed-size, all machine-made quilt, and it presented unique challenges at every step of the process. This quilt has been honored with multiple prestigious awards.

# CHAPTER 2

# Recording Inspiration

*The desire to create is one of the deepest yearnings of the human soul.*
*… We each have an inherent wish to create something that did not exist before.*
*… The more you trust and rely upon … [inspiration], the greater your capacity to create.*
—*Dieter F. Uchtdorf*

## Inspiration   *noun*

1. something that stimulates the human mind to creative thought or to the making of art
2. somebody or something that inspires somebody
3. the quality of being stimulated to creative thought or activity, or the manifestation of this
4. a sudden brilliant idea
5. divine guidance and influence on human beings

Just like "a goal that isn't written down is only a dream," inspiration for a quilt is lost if you don't sketch it. How many times have you had a brilliant idea for a quilt and later couldn't remember any of the details because you never sketched it out? Recording inspiration for a quilt not only creates a compilation of ideas that you come across, it also includes design ideas for a specific quilt, making a concrete history of that quilt.

# A Word about Creativity and Designing Quilts

Creative ideas often come when you're alone—driving in the car, in the shower, lying awake in the quiet of the night when you wish you could sleep. I don't know why that is. Perhaps that is the time when we can actually listen to ourselves—when we're not engaged with other people. Creativity is very personal. I have an inherent need to create beautiful things; I'm compelled to do it.

Many people *think* they aren't the least bit creative—like my mom. She didn't paint, do crafts, or play an instrument, and she followed recipes to a T. Yet she was a gifted decorator in the home and knew just how to place each piece of furniture and décor to maximize familial interaction. Creative.

The one absurd statement that always makes me laugh is, "I can't take an art class. I don't know how to draw." An art class would be the very environment in which you could start that learning process!

After the fall of the Berlin Wall, a West German teacher gave a group of East German grade school students paper and a pencil and a simple instruction: Draw something. The students sat quietly for a few minutes and did not move. The teacher asked them to proceed with their drawings, but still the students didn't move. When asked why they weren't drawing, the students replied, "Tell us what we should draw." They were used to being told what to draw: a house or a tree or a bird. When told to use their own creativity, they simply didn't know what that was or understand that they were free to draw whatever they wished. The instruction simply did not compute.

The biggest block to creativity is unwillingness to take a risk, also known as a lack of self-confidence. We sometimes don't dare take a risk because we feel that we might look foolish, and we want to look great. No one is going to start a quilt without believing that he or she can make the quilt. Start by believing that you can do it and that the outcome will be worth it.

In his book *Free Play: Improvisation in Life and Art*, Stephen Nachmanovitch states that the essence of creativity is improvisation—the process of creating something without any preparation or instructions to follow. Sometimes we have to start with the thought "This may not work," but that can be where our best ideas come from.

Einstein said, "If at first, the idea is not absurd, then there is no hope for it." We have to climb out on that tree branch or jump off that step to get going—to give ourselves permission to do something without someone else's instructions.

It's like wanting to create a flower for a piece of appliqué, and rather than turning to a book or magazine to find a pattern, taking a photo of a flower that you like and drawing your own shape.

Too hard, you say? Many fine artists use photographs rather than live models to create their paintings. Is that cheating? No, it's not. It's an aid to help your brain remember the image you want to put to paper, canvas, or fabric.

"I don't know how to draw," you say? You know how to write in cursive style, don't you? Drawing simple appliqué shapes is the same as making larger cursive curves, or doodles. If you're a doodler, you're already closer to being an artist. Talented quilt artist Lura Schwarz Smith suggests that her students keep a daily drawing journal, because the more you practice drawing, the better you will get.

I was not raised in an artistically nurturing environment. I nurtured my own desire to create art and clothing myself. Inspiration for what I create comes from another source outside my own ability. The direction of my work is greatly inspired by the beauty of nature and the source of life. And I practice every day.

# A Digital Camera Is Your Best Quilting Tool

Before the advent of digital cameras, I loved to use a Polaroid camera that gave me "instant" pictures. I could capture a shape that I wanted to remember or view a quilt's layout to make sure it was balanced.

Now that our cameras give us instant gratification—photos that can be erased if they're blurry instead of being processed into snapshots—we can take pictures of everything we want without the cost of developing.

I take my camera with me wherever I go to collect images that will be useful to me for quilt design. I use the images for inspiration when I need to design a quilt, a block, or an element for a quilt.

Downloading the files from your camera to your computer will allow you to pick and choose design elements to play with using your favorite software, or to sketch on paper.

# Design Journals

I love to use handmade journals to collect the inspiration that comes my way. Capturing inspirational designs in a journal is a sure way to keep them organized and handy. You can put your hands on them when you need them. I also use composition books—they are inexpensive and easy to find.

I have lined pages, gridded pages, and three-subject notebooks that I use interchangeably. I sketch, draw, note, glue, and staple a multitude of design sources and fabrics into my journals.

I choose a focus fabric, taking care to save the color print dots in the selvage to match fabrics to. I cut a 3" × 4" swatch of both the focus fabric and the background fabric. Using a larger piece of background fabric allows me to audition any supporting fabric from my palette to see how it will work on the background. Then I find the supporting fabrics—the colors of the palette that vary in print size, texture, and value—and cut a 1" × 1" square

of each. I glue all the fabrics to a page by color and then by value, so I have my fabric choices at a glance. With those fabrics glued into the book, I take my journal along as I shop in different locations for fabric to make sure that I'm filling in what my needs are and not being driven by desire, and that I'm not purchasing the same fabric again.

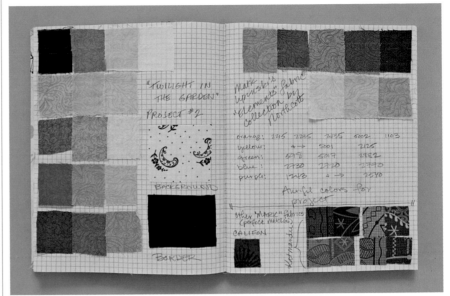

I sketch—in pencil, never in pen—any design that comes to my mind. I might use it, I might refine it, or I might keep it for future reference. In any case, it's there when I need it. I use a pencil, which allows me to erase lines I don't need or change or add an element without having to redraw.

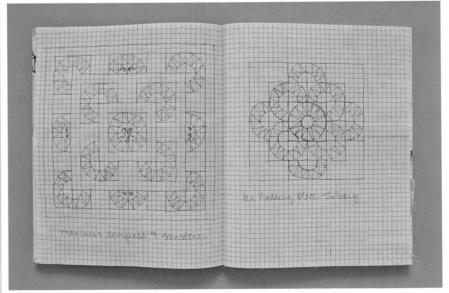

Sketching an idea allows you to play with design, balance, and placement.

# Your Secret Story

This last issue is almost the most important reason to record your inspiration.

Consider this: As contemporary (meaning "now") quilters, we place ultimate value on labeling our quilt so that in the future, people will know that we made that quilt. Okay, so they'll know our name, where we lived, when we made the quilt, and what it was made out of. But what about the story—our secret story, that only we know—about what we were feeling and working out, and what was going on in our family, in the community, in the world, and how those things affected us and how we made our quilts. Our quilts are so dependent upon our tactile relationship with them: how soothing it is to handle our fabrics and how we thoughtfully go about cutting and carefully stitching each piece. We quilters often comment that quilting is cheaper than therapy, and we really do use our quilting as a form of comfort.

*In Elly Sienkiewicz's book,* Baltimore Album Revival!, *one quilter expressed her feelings about her quilt this way: "The quilt and I have been through some difficult times. I will remember the sadness and pain, but also the joy, excitement, and satisfaction I had in making it."*

—Ruth H. Meyers, Dhahran, Saudi Arabia

Those two sentences hold a deeper, much larger story of the quilt and the quilter—a personal story that is not for everyone's eyes. But what about the quilter's family and those who know her and love her—especially after she is gone? My biggest regret when my mom died was in looking at her high school yearbooks and wanting to ask her what she did in high school and to explain what the inscriptions from her friends meant. Those stories of my mom are forever lost, but if she had kept a journal or written a life history, I would know much more about the private side of my mom. I know, by looking at my own quilts, all the personal stories that they each hold. If I don't write them down, they will be lost with me.

So what is your story in each of your quilts? Have you ever just looked at the fabrics and the pattern and gone on a little memory tour of sorts? I did that with a Log Cabin quilt that I made in 1986, when my daughter was entering kindergarten. I used a peach fabric with French geese on it to make her first-day-of-school dress. I then used the leftovers in my Log Cabin quilt. Halfway through the school year, my husband was laid off from his job, and changes ensued. There is so much family history in that quilt, including the one ink spot that I have never been able to get out, caused when my son laid a permanent pen on the quilt and the ink wicked into the fabric. I was pretty upset at the time. Now that my son is a grown man with a child on the way, I love to see that ink stain and remember when he was little and loved to sit on my lap, wrapped up in that quilt after getting out of the pool.

That story may not be meaningful to an anonymous observer, but it's a very important story for my children, who are fighting over who gets that quilt when I pass away!

How cool would it be to begin your quilt in a journal and add to the story as you go? While you're working on the quilt, add the pictures and details that reflect your private story of feelings, hopes, and wishes that you want to share as a part of your life history. It will certainly make writing your life history much easier when the time comes, if you desire to do so.

One of Annie's "secret stories"

# A Note about Copyright

Because I'm a designer, I take special care not to copy a quilt that someone else has designed, no matter how much I like it, and I'm keenly aware of copyright infringement.

We have to be careful with other design elements that we find and desire to put into our quilts. Thinking that you can change five different elements in someone else's design and then it becomes your own is a major fallacy—and *is* a copyright violation. Changing someone else's design is adapting the work, and only the copyright holder has the right to adapt his or her own design.

If you see a really great design in a carpet in a hotel hallway, someone designed it and owns the copyright to it. If you see a really sweet flower on a greeting card, someone designed it and owns the copyright to it. You must be careful not to copy someone else's work.

If you want to make a quilt from someone else's pattern or use a block from someone else's design in a new quilt that you are designing, you need the creator's permission to add it to your work—especially if you will show the quilt publicly. A simple letter or a phone call, asking for permission, is obligatory. Don't be afraid that the copyright holder will want to charge you a ridiculous amount of money—usually all the designer wants is for you to acknowledge him or her in the credits. If you are copying from someone else, the last (and worst) thing you can do is to pretend that it was your original idea.

If you want to make sure that your designs are uniquely yours, find a beautiful rose in a garden. Draw your impression of the rose and use it in your quilt without worrying that someone designed it and owns a copyright to it!

# CHAPTER 3

# Choosing Fabrics for Appliqué

*It's not easy being green.* —*Kermit the Frog*

## Choice   *noun*

**1.** a decision to choose one thing in preference to others
**2.** the chance or ability to choose between different things
**3.** a variety of things or possibilities from which to choose
**4.** the best or most desirable part

Avocado green, lime green, kelly green, moss green, blue-green, forest green—how do you choose your fabrics for a quilt anyway? Choosing fabrics is the quilter's most difficult challenge.

Choosing fabrics is another one of those skills that needs to be practiced to get it right. First, we must decide on the color; then, there are other determining factors in the selection.

What? Wait—did you say that we need to consider *more* than color when choosing fabrics? Absolutely! Choosing our fabrics isn't only about what colors we want to use; that's just where we *begin*. Our biggest problem with choosing fabrics isn't that we don't understand color—we all know which colors we like and want to use. Didn't you pick the paint colors in your home, and don't you have a favorite color?

We haven't lived in a black-and-white world since before Walt Disney's *Wonderful World of Color*—and, well, we didn't back then either. In Audrey Hepburn's movie *Funny Face,* they sang about "Think Pink." I lived in a pink house with a pink bedroom and a kitchen with pink appliances.

Our world is dominated by color trends. Just look around you. We live our lives by color trends that are chosen for us by an international committee, and these colors affect our clothing, our homes, and even our quilting.

When we make a quilt for someone else, we choose our fabrics based on that person's color preferences. When we make a quilt for our home, we make it based on the colors of the room where the quilt will reside. We know what colors we like. If our quilts come out not quite the way we want them to, it's usually not that our workmanship is bad, our points aren't pointy, or our seams don't align—it's because there is something wrong with our fabric choices.

## The Key to Your Fabric Choices

The biggest problem we have in choosing fabrics for a quilt is that we don't understand that there is another element to choosing fabrics *besides* color.

Have you ever thought about *the value of fabric*? No, it's not how much it costs. Value is the lightness or darkness of the color of the fabric and is the *key* to choosing all the fabrics for your quilts. Value will help separate the pieces of fabric so viewers can see a distinct pattern in the quilt. Value gives quilts shadows and light, and allows elements to come forward or go back, creating a three-dimensional effect. When your designs fall flat and disappear, it's because the fabrics are too close in value, not because the colors are wrong.

Before we can talk about choosing fabrics, we must understand color fundamentals:

The pure color is the *hue*.

When white is added to the hue, it becomes a *tint*—or is lighter.

When black is added to the hue, it becomes a *shade*—or is darker.

When gray is added to the hue, it becomes a *tone*—or is muted.

When tinting and shading are done in steps or degrees, it's called a *gradation*, as shown below.

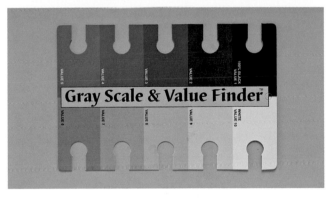

The degrees of value that quilters use are as follows:

Light

Medium light

Medium

Medium dark

Dark

Do you notice a similarity in that list? Three of the five values are mediums—and then you wonder why you have a problem choosing fabrics! But each of the five values plays an important role and can be very distinct, as the next photos show.

If you look at the first sentence of this chapter, you will realize that the different colors are listed from light to dark. That's how you need to start looking at fabrics—by color and then by value. So if you are going to use pinks and greens, you will use pinks ranging from pale pink to maroon and greens ranging from avocado to forest green.

Our stumbling block as quilters is that the fabrics that are designed for us are too close in value—mostly medium values because those are the fabrics that are eye-catching and appealing. We have very few darks and even fewer lights to choose from. Fabrics that are too close in value will "gray out" together and blend into each other so they look like one fabric, disappearing either within themselves or into the background. That is how we lose the design of the pieced block or the distinction of the appliquéd flower.

# Start with a Focus Fabric

I like to use a focus fabric as my color palette and then choose supporting fabrics from that palette. A focus fabric is a beautiful print with an assortment of colors that you can use to choose additional fabrics. A focus fabric is not a one-color fabric whose print you like—that type of fabric is a monochromatic print and is actually a supporting fabric.

## Look at the Focus Fabric Samples

Each focus fabric sample is a distinct print with a range of colors. Most fabrics have little color dots along the selvage to show you how many colors were used and in what order they were printed on the fabric. The dots may even give you a hint about value, as each color gets lighter on the selvage. To choose the additional fabrics for your quilt, look for fabrics in each of those colors. Then choose additional fabrics in those color ranges that are lighter and darker than the first ones you chose.

When I save fabric swatches in my design journal, I cut the focus fabric so it includes the color dots on the selvage. I take it with me when I select fabrics.

# Determining Value

There are some nifty "tools" that you can use to determine the value of fabric.

**Your Eyes Are Your Best Tool**   Squinting assists in cutting out the overhead light and allows you to view the lightness and darkness of fabrics and quilts more clearly. You have to squint tightly to determine the value, and it helps to squint from a distance.

**Use a Copier**   Place your fabrics on a copier and make a black-and-white copy.

**Use Your Camera**   Through the viewfinder, you get a clearer picture of the values. Take a picture of the fabrics and look at it. You will see the values of your fabric selections much more clearly in the photo.

**Use a Reducing Glass or Security Peephole from the Hardware Store**   The view through a reducing glass or peephole will put what you're looking at 20–30 feet away from you. The distance helps you see value more clearly.

**Use a Design Wall**   Pin your fabrics up on a design wall and stand back as far as you can to view the fabrics. When we view fabrics close up, our eyes fool us, and all we see is the color and print of the fabric. If you stand back and view from a distance, I guarantee you that you will be able to determine the value more easily. To have this theory work right, stand at least six feet away from your fabric.

No design wall? A bulletin board works well, as does affixing fabric with blue low-tack painter's tape to a wall, door, mirror, or window.

**Stack the Fabrics against a Wall and Move Back**   Don't look at your fabrics for color, but to make sure that you have enough variety in the values.

**Take Off Your Glasses**   If you wear glasses, take them off to view the fabric. If everything looks blurry, that's good—it will really allow you to see the value better than when you have your glasses on!

**View Fabrics through Red Plexiglas**   Also known as a Ruby Beholder, this tool can be helpful except when you're viewing red. The red plastic cancels out the red in the fabric and makes it look white. You'll need to use a piece of green Plexiglas to view the reds, and that will make the greens look white. Painters and artists use several colors of Plexiglas, which aid in finding the values of a variety of colors. These can be found at art supply stores.

# Playing with Fabric

I love to play with fabric, creating all sorts of realistic-looking flowers, leaves, and appliqué elements.

This rose is in the folk garden border of *Gran's Memory Quilt* (see page 61).

Hand-dyed and batik fabrics have wonderful pools of dye that are darker, or change color, to make wonderful rose petals.

When selecting fabrics for appliqué, I use mostly printed fabrics. I love the nuances of prints, especially those that look like solids from a distance but give viewers a surprise when they look at the quilt up close. You can get shadows and light using prints also.

## Using Your Fabrics to Mimic Nature

Seeing how light hits an object, and mirroring that in your appliqué, will make your quilt outstanding. If you're not sure what that looks like, look out the window. Depending on the particular position of the sun in the sky, light will hit part of an object, leaving another part, usually the underside, in shadow. Mimicking shadows and light with our fabric choices gives our appliqué dimension.

To use fabrics to create realistic flowers and foliage, consider these rules of nature:

- Stems are always darker, as they are in the shade, under leaves and flowers.

- Leaves are always darker at the bottom of the stem.

- Top leaves are lighter because the sun hits them.

- Leaves in between the top and bottom are in the medium value range.

- The centers of flowers aren't always yellow, nor are they light.

- The tips of flower petals are lighter than the insides of the petals that meet the center.

- Don't make layered flowers look like they are bull's-eyes.

- The base of a vase is darker than the bowl of the vase.

- "Fussy place" (page 39) fusible leaf and petal shapes strategically so they are darker at the base and lighter at the tip.

# What Works, What Doesn't Work

This series of photos will help you choose fabrics for your appliqué pieces.

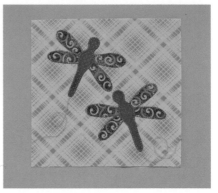

Values are too close on the left—the dragonfly wings disappear into the background. Values are just right on the right.

See the "bull's-eye" effect in the flower on the left? Not very appealing. Better to blend the flower values from light to dark, to the inside or to the outside of the flower.

The background fabric has too much movement, so the eye has no place to rest. A quieter, more subdued print would be better.

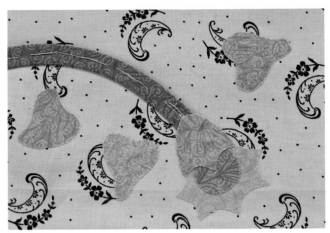

On this test piece, the background that I thought was perfect is good for some of the elements but too busy for others. The yellow flowers and light green leaves fade into the background, and the paisleys in the background fabric attach themselves to the appliqué elements in an unattractive way.

When choosing fabrics, remember that if you look at them while working at your tabletop, it will be difficult to determine the value because they are so close to you. Use the tools and ideas listed on page 23 to help choose correctly.

# A Postscript about Focus Fabric

You don't have to use your focus fabric in the quilt top! You can use it as your color palette only. For instance, my *Flora Bella* quilt (page 70) has none of the focus fabric in the appliqué. I loved that the print and the colors were the exact ones I wanted to use: magenta, purple, orange, yellow, and green on a black background. The harder I tried to work the focus fabric in to one of the appliqué designs, the more apparent it became that it didn't belong there. The quilt told me what it wanted, and I had to obey, so I used the focus fabric as the backing because I loved it so much. It always surprises quilters to find that they don't have to use their focus fabrics in their quilts.

*Flora Bella* focus fabric (now the backing)

# CHAPTER 4

# Tools and Supplies for Appliqué

*Your equipment does not affect the quality of your image. The less time and effort you spend worrying about your equipment the more time and effort you can spend creating great images. The right equipment just makes it easier, faster or more convenient for you to get the results you need.*

—Ken Rockwell

## Equipment *noun*

1. the tools, clothing, or other items needed for a particular purpose or activity

2. the intellectual and emotional resources that enable a person to succeed at a task or role in life

3. the equipping of somebody or something with what is necessary for a particular purpose or activity

### BASIC SUPPLIES
1. Thread to match fabrics
2. Pencil with a sharp point
3. Small, sharp fabric scissors
4. Eraser
5. Iron
6. Spray starch
7. Iron cleaner
8. Ironing board
9. Rotary cutter and replacement blades
10. Rotary cutting mat
11. Ruler
12. Tweezers
13. Design wall
14. Bias tape maker
15. Flexible ruler
16. Stiletto
17. Marking tools
18. Low-tack tape

### MACHINE APPLIQUÉ SUPPLIES
19. Extra bobbins and a bobbin holder
20. Sharp machine needles
21. Self-threading needles
22. Paper-backed fusible web
23. Tracing copy paper
24. Thread snips
25. Ball-head pins
26. Seam ripper
27. Open-toe appliqué foot
28. Open-toe darning foot
29. Quarter-inch-seam foot
30. Lightbox
31. Appliqué pressing sheet

### HAND APPLIQUÉ SUPPLIES
32. Freezer paper
33. Piece of cardboard
34. Paper-cutting scissors
35. Gluestick
36. Appliqué glue
37. Silk thread
38. Appliqué needles
39. Clear fingernail polish
40. Sheet protector
41. Disposable kitchen cutting mat
42. Paper towels
43. Small, moist sponge in a dish
44. Thread Heaven
45. Thimble
46. Needle threader

# Basic Supplies

## Thread to match fabrics

Cotton thread is desirable for my method of machine appliqué. I use Mettler 50-weight and Aurifil Mako 28-weight for appliqué and Aurifil 50-weight for piecing. Use a good-quality thread that is not old—meaning don't use a thread that is on a wooden spool from your mother's 1945 sewing box. Purchase new threads that match, or contrast with, your fabrics. When choosing thread to match a fabric, pull the thread out and lay it on the fabric, rather than holding the spool of thread next to or on top of the fabric.

You will want to use a neutral thread to piece your entire quilt.

 **Note** If you use black fabrics as the background, always use black thread to piece sections together. Using even a dark gray will appear lighter than the fabric and show up when you least expect it.

## Pencil with a sharp point

Use a lead pencil with a sharp point to mark the fusible web. You can use either a 2/HB wood pencil or a mechanical pencil. If you use a wood pencil, keep an inexpensive motorized pencil sharpener nearby to keep your pencil sharp. I also like keeping a good eraser handy, as my pencil erasers always disappear before my lead runs out.

## Small, sharp fabric scissors

It's harder to cut small pieces with large scissors, so you will want to use a nice small pair of scissors that cut down to the point. My favorites are Clover Patchwork/Cutwork Scissors and EK Success Cutter Bees. You will need to get into small pointy places with your appliqué scissors.

Another good solution for cutting fusible web shapes is to use a swivel-head craft knife—but you must be careful not to trim too close to the drawn line. Using a craft knife takes more precision than does using good sharp scissors.

## Eraser

As I design, I tend to erase my pencil lines a fair bit. If I sketch incorrectly, I can erase my mistakes. After I draw final, permanent lines on my pattern, I erase all the pencil lines so I have a clean pattern.

## Iron

An iron is an essential tool for machine appliqué—and quilting in general. Your iron doesn't have to be expensive, but it should have a good steam feature and maintain a consistent temperature. I've had irons that spit water instead of steam, don't heat up high enough, or heat up too high. I had a very expensive sewing iron that heated up too high, didn't have auto-shutoff, and scorched my fabrics. Nowadays, I look for the best inexpensive iron I can find at a discount retail store because I am quite hard on my irons. When my kids were little, my irons were always being dropped, and once they're dropped, they become door-stops because they are unreliable.

So I look for an iron that has a good soleplate, holes for steam, auto-shutoff, and that's about it.

## Spray starch

Starch is used to stabilize the background fabric for machine appliqué. I prefer to use what I can find on sale at the grocery store because I use lots of it. I prefer regular weight over heavyweight, as it's easier to add starch than remove it. Also, sizing is not starch. Sizing doesn't have the bonding agent that starch has.

## Iron cleaner

Iron cleaner is an essential supply when working with fusible web. Keep the soleplate clean to avoid fusible residue getting on your work.

## Ironing board

A good sturdy ironing board is essential for the methods of hand and machine appliqué presented in this book. I prefer using a full-size ironing board for blocks and borders and a tabletop ironing board for preparing appliqué shapes. If I had to choose one, I would use the full-size ironing board and adjust it to table height so I could sit while working.

## Rotary cutter and replacement blades

I cut all the fabric for blocks, sashing, cornerstones, borders, bias stems, and bindings with my trusty rotary cutter—a quilter's best friend. Keep extra rotary blades handy so you can change them when they become dull. Dull blades are more likely to cut you than sharp ones, as you bear down harder on the cutter when it's not cutting through all the layers. I buy my blades in a five-pack and keep two boxes: one that I mark "New" and one that is marked "Old." I throw the entire "Old" box away when it's full and make a new one.

## Rotary cutting mat

A rotary cutting mat is also an essential tool for every quilter. Use the correct size of mat for the project that you are working on. A 12″ × 18″ mat isn't going to work if you're cutting large pieces. I like to use the largest green mat, 24″ × 36″, to cover my work area and keep it clean. I use the back (nonprinted) side of the mat and rely on the measurements on my rulers rather than the lines on the mat. Mats expand and contract with heat, so they aren't always consistent for measuring. Keep your mat out of the heat of your car (where it will warp like a vinyl record) and don't allow your kids to put the pizza that has just been delivered on top of it either (a hazard of working on the dinner table—I know this by experience).

If you discover that something hot has been placed on your mat, remove the hot item and simply run your hands quickly over the mat, flattening it, until it completely cools off. Your mat will be nice and flat again.

## Ruler

Acrylic rulers are the only type to use for quilting, but which one is the proper size? I have a variety of sizes and use the ruler that best fits the size of the project. I always use a ruler to measure fabric rather than using the printed grid on my cutting mat, so my measurements are consistent. I have even gone to a plastic store to have rulers cut that are longer than standard rulers for special projects that need a larger size. I also have 17″ and 18″ plastic squares that I use to cut larger appliqué blocks.

## Tweezers

Sometimes it's hard to hold onto things that are tiny—like little appliqué shapes or the ends of threads that need to be cut. Tweezers help grab those things.

## Design wall

I personally believe that a design wall is the greatest tool a quilter can have to help him or her see the "big picture" while constructing a quilt. If you can preview your fabric choices on the design wall, keep your in-progress block up so you can mull it over as you make it, and then display the finished block for all to see, you will be more satisfied with the finished quilt. If you can pick the fabrics for your subsequent blocks while viewing the fabric choices you've already made, you can make sure that you're duplicating fabrics only when you want to.

To me, a design wall is an essential tool for every quilter. Putting your work up on a wall parallel to the upright position of your head helps you see the work correctly. After all, we view quilts at a quilt show that way, don't we? We don't look at them on the bed, on the living room floor, or draped on a sofa.

Design walls don't have to be expensive, and they don't have to be permanent. I have used a piece of batting pinned to a wall and quilt blocks taped to a wall of mirrors at a retreat.

## Bias tape maker

If you want to make bias strips quickly and easily, a bias tape maker is a good solution.

## Flexible ruler

A flexible ruler is a great tool for creating curves that are just the right length, and then being able to make them again on the pattern without losing the curve.

## Stiletto

A stiletto is like a seam ripper, but with only one really sharp point. It allows you to move pieces into place or hold pieces down while stitching. Keep it covered with the protector cap when not in use.

## Marking tools

I use Roxanne Quilter's Choice Chalk Marking Pencils. They come in white and silver. For machine quilting, use a Clover fine white marking pen, which disappears when the mark is heated with an iron. I use a pen-type stylus with tracing copy paper.

## Low-tack painter's tape

This tape is an essential tool in my arsenal of quilting supplies and can be found at any home improvement store in the paint aisle. *Low-tack* means that it comes off surfaces easily, without tearing or pulling. I use it to tape trash bags to the edge of a worktable; I tape blocks to a window or mirror when a design wall isn't available; I write on it and affix it to a block or quilt part to remind me of something I need to do; I tape designs to a window for easy transfer onto fabric—and dozens of other uses.

# Machine Appliqué Supplies

### Extra bobbins and a bobbin holder

You need an extra bobbin for each thread color that you use in your appliqué project. The bobbin thread needs to match the top thread so there aren't little dots of a different color on the top of your beautiful work. A bobbin holder will keep the bobbins organized and reserved for that specific use while you work on your project.

## Sharp machine needles

I prefer Schmetz Microtex 80/12 needles, which just seem to work best for me. The 80/12 size matches the weight of the cotton thread I use.

## Self-threading needles

These hand-sewing needles are a lifesaver. The needle has a split in the top that allows you to pop the thread into the eye, which saves time threading the needle. You will use this needle to bury your thread ends for tying off on the back, so keep it near your sewing machine.

## Paper-backed fusible web

Fusible web is a very thin sheet of glue that is heat sensitive and backed by paper. The glue melts at a certain temperature. All fusibles come with manufacturer's directions. Take a moment to read the directions so you know how long to iron the fusible to your fabric to make the glue adhere. Be careful when ironing the fusible to keep it away from surfaces that you don't want it attaching to.

Most fusible web comes on a bolt and needs to be cut. Fusible is delicate. Don't roll or fold and crease the fusible, or allow the sales clerk who is cutting it for you to roll or fold it either. Cut the fusible into sheets and store it in gallon-size re-sealable plastic zipper bags. I mark mine with the type of fusible and the date that I prepared the bag so I will remember.

Fusible will not stick to surfaces in areas where there is high humidity. I had a student call me from her vacation in St. Thomas, wailing because her appliqué pieces wouldn't stick no matter how much she ironed them. Then, she explained that the labels were falling off her hair products. Don't try to machine appliqué in the tropics! Hand appliqué instead.

 **All Fusible Web Is Not Created Equal!** The essential notion for fine machine appliqué is paper-backed fusible web. It is used to trace appliqué designs cleanly and adhere the appliqué elements to the background fabric in preparation for stitching. A fusible web without paper backing would not be a good choice for my method of machine appliqué.

You need a delicate fusible for the appliqué that I feature in this book; my recommendation for the best fusible available is Soft Fuse. It performs perfectly for fine machine appliqué—better than the other brands that I have tested and used previously.

The paper backing on Soft Fuse enables you to trace appliqué designs accurately with a pencil and cut them with a clean edge. Also, the glue is not sticky and will not gum up your machine needle.

If you can't find Soft Fuse at your local quilt shop, you can purchase it online (see Resources, page 156).

## Tracing copy paper

The only tracing paper I use for appliqué is Clover Chacopy paper. It is a chalk-based paper that isn't messy like carbon paper and can be brushed off, similar to Saral paper. I use it with a tracing stylus to mark placement lines when I don't have a lightbox handy.

## Thread snips

My favorite snips are made by Havel. The curved, short blade of these snips lets you clip appliqué threads without clipping into the appliqué.

## Ball-head pins

A pin is better than just your fingers for moving pieces into place. The pin grabs hold of the top layer of fabric (the appliqué shape) so you can move it into place easily. Ball-head pins are easier to hold than traditional flat-top pins. You can also use a pin to hold the appliqué piece down while stitching, similar to using a stiletto.

## Seam ripper

Sometimes you need it.

## Open-toe appliqué foot

This foot is completely open so you have a clear view of how and where your machine is stitching. It helps you align the stitches with the curve of the appliqué while you're stitching along the inside of the foot.

An open-toe foot doesn't have a clear bar across the front, because even a clear bar will impede your view. You can cut the bar off (with no structural damage to the foot) with a pair of wire-cutter pliers.

## Open-toe darning foot

An open-toe darning foot will enable you to add thread embellishment to your appliqué. The foot sits above the throat plate and allows you to move the fabric smoothly by hand underneath the foot. The open toe allows you to see where you are stitching the design. Always remember to lower the feed dogs when doing thread embellishment.

## Quarter-inch-seam foot

This foot has a ¼" guide bar on the right side of the foot so your seam allowance will always be accurate.

## Lightbox

This comes in handy for tracing placement lines onto starched background fabric.

## Appliqué pressing sheet

You may want to use an appliqué pressing sheet—or not.

A pressing sheet will protect your iron, fabric, and ironing board, but I'm always afraid that a pressing sheet will adjust the layers of my appliqués while I'm pressing them—when I don't want them to move.

Also, pressing sheets make the heat of the iron more intense, creating the chance of over-fusing. If excess fusible comes out from under the appliqué shapes, which is often the case as the fusible melts, it will collect on the sheet and then transfer itself to your next set of appliqués or to an area of the background that is not meant to show glue.

Finally, you must wait to remove the appliqué until it's cool on the sheet. If you remove it while it's still hot, the shape will distort, and you'll have to make a new one.

# Hand Appliqué Supplies

## Freezer paper

Freezer paper can be found at the grocery store in the food-wrap aisle. One box will last a long time.

## Piece of cardboard

You can recycle a piece of cardboard from a wrapped garment or the back of a tablet of paper. It should be a single thickness, not corrugated.

## Paper-cutting scissors

I use Cutter Bee scissors that are clearly marked "paper cutting only."

## Gluestick

Avery Dennison brand, which can be found at a quilt shop or office supply store, is my favorite. A clean, moist gluestick works best. I keep mine in the refrigerator until I'm ready to use it, and then I put it back. When the glue is cold, it's nice and firm and doesn't make glue "threads" when you pull the gluestick away from the piece.

## Appliqué glue

I prefer Appli-Glue by Jillily Studio or Roxanne Glue-Baste-It appliqué glue. Roxanne offers a small bottle that is handy for travel.

## Silk thread

For hand appliqué, I use YLI brand 100-weight silk thread in neutral colors (224, 226, 235, and 242). The thread completely disappears when I stitch, and the thread color doesn't show, so I don't worry about matching the thread to the color of my fabrics—I just match it to the value of the fabrics.

## Appliqué needles

For hand appliqué, my favorite needles are Roxanne brand sharps, #10 or #11.

## Clear fingernail polish

Every once in a while, you will have a fray that just won't lie down no matter what you do. If you dab it with a tiny amount of clear nail polish and push it into place, it will stay. Let the fabric dry before resuming work.

## Sheet protector

The clear type of protector that you use to hold a sheet of paper in a binder works best. I place the sheet protector on top of my pattern to keep the glue off the pattern while I am aligning the appliqué elements in their places.

## Disposable kitchen cutting mat

These can be found at discount retail stores in packs of four. They are smooth on both sides. Glue is easily cleaned off them, and I use them as a work surface.

## Paper towels

Use the lint-free type for drying your hands, the stiletto, and any surface that has been wiped clean of glue.

## Small, moist sponge in a dish

This is useful for wiping glue off your fingers, the stiletto, and work surfaces. It also works for removing threads from the end of the gluestick.

## Thread Heaven

This thread conditioner comes in a little blue box. Run the thread over the top of the conditioner, and then knot.

## Thimble

I always use a thimble to protect the finger that pushes the needle when hand sewing. If the thimble fits correctly, you should be able to feel the inside cap of the thimble on the tip of your finger, and the thimble should stay on your finger when you shake your hand lightly.

## Needle threader

A desktop needle threader comes in handy when it gets tough to thread a needle. Insert the eye of the needle into the threader, lay a piece of thread in the groove, push the plunger, and—by magic—you have a threaded needle.

# CHAPTER 5

# Appliqué Methods

*It is a token of healthy and gentle characteristics when women of high thoughts and accomplishments love to sew; especially as they are never more at home with their own hearts than while so occupied.* —Nathaniel Hawthorne

> **Appliqué** *noun*
>
> **1.** shaped pieces of fabric sewn on a foundation fabric to form a design or pattern

## Machine Appliqué

I love the folk-art nature of appliqué quilts and Baltimore Album style. I prefer to appliqué using the stitched raw-edge fusible technique because it is a time-saving, no-nonsense way to achieve beautiful and precise results. This method is a great choice for those who wish to make beautiful, intricate appliqué without doing it by hand.

The method I use removes the center of the fusible web from the appliqué shape so there is no stiffness or buildup of fusible web that would create thickness. Instead, the appliqué is soft and the quilt less heavy—appearing more like hand appliqué. Viewers of quilts appliquéd in this way always try to guess whether the blanket stitch used for the quilt was done by machine or by hand, and find it hard to believe that it was made with fusible web.

 **Note** Prewashed fabrics work best with this technique. Fusible web adheres best to prewashed fabrics.

## Let's Begin!

Before beginning any project, make sure you have a brand-new needle in your sewing machine. Use a full bobbin of thread that matches the color of the thread in the top spool. Stitch a little on a scrap piece of fabric to make sure your machine is making the right stitch and not skipping or bunching.

 **Tip** Always check the tension on your sample to ensure that the bobbin thread isn't showing on the top of the sample and that the top thread isn't coming to the back. If the tension doesn't appear even on both sides, refer to your sewing machine manual to adjust either the top tension or the screw on the bobbin case that will adjust the bobbin tension.

## Make a Test Stitch Sample

You need the following materials:

4" × 8" piece of neutral-colored scrap fabric

Medium-value thread with matching bobbin

Open-toe appliqué foot

Permanent marking pen

Fold the fabric, wrong sides together, and press a crease with your thumbnail.

At the crease, fold a ½" tuck and finger-press flat—this will look like you are appliquéing the tuck to the background fabric.

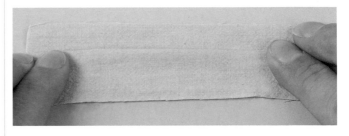

Choose the stitch you would like to use (see Stitch Selection, page 42) and make a sample stitch along the tuck, starting with the straight stitch in the background and the zig of the stitch going into the tuck.

Make the first set of stitches to see how the stitch performs, and then make additional tucks in the sample fabric and adjust the stitch until you like the look of it. The stitch should measure ⅛" wide and ⅛" long.

Use a permanent pen to write the stitch settings onto the fabric beside the stitch you like best; include the stitch number, stitch width, stitch length, and whether you need to set the needle position all the way to the right to line up the needle along the inside of the foot. I always add a right arrow for "needle in the rightmost position" and a down arrow for "needle-down position" because my machine gives me the choice to set those.

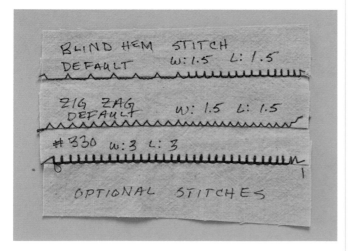

*Correct stitching:* The straight stitch is butting right up against the tuck (appliqué shape), with the zig going into the tuck (appliqué shape).

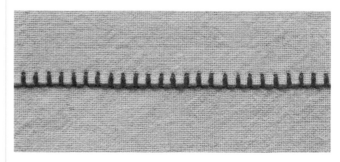

*Incorrect stitching:* The straight stitch is too far away from the tuck (appliqué shape), allowing the background fabric to show within the stitch and the zig to hang off onto the background.

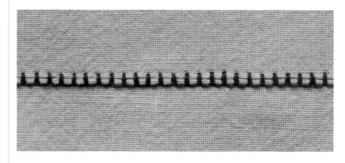

*Incorrect stitching:* The straight stitch comes up onto the tuck (appliqué shape), so you can see the edge of the tuck outside the straight stitch and the shape is not framed properly.

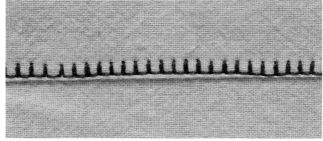

Keep your stitch sample handy so you will always know what settings to use to set up your sewing machine, especially if you don't have a memory feature on your machine that will save the stitch for future use.

Once you have the stitch set the way you like it, you're ready to make an appliqué sample set.

## Make a Sample of Simple Shapes

These appliqué shapes—a stacked flower and simple leaf—are perfect examples of the edges you will stitch on your appliqué, including points, soft curves, hard curves, and inverted points. Practice these before beginning your first project.

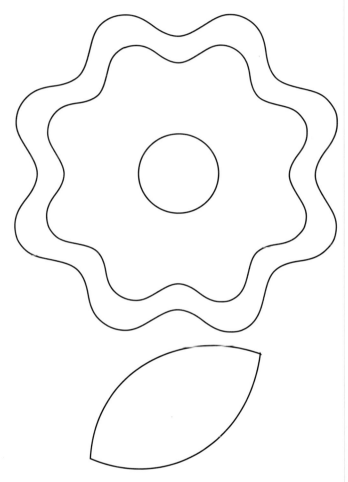

Simple Shapes: Flower and Leaf Patterns

Completed flower

Assemble the needed supplies (see pages 26–32) along with a 6″ × 6″ piece of starched background fabric and small pieces of fabric to make the flower and leaf.

## Tracing Appliqué Patterns onto Fusible Web

Using the patterns at left, trace the appliqué shapes onto the paper side of a sheet of fusible web using a sharp pencil.

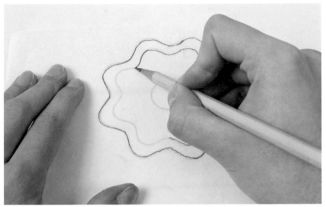

Trace each of the individual appliqué shapes separately. Trace the stacked shapes, such as this flower, in one unit, as shown.

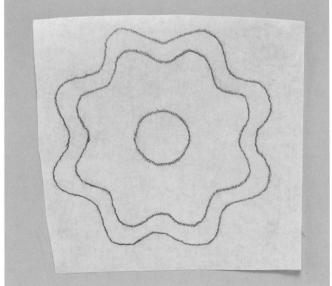

## Cutting the Outline of the Appliqué Shape from Fusible Web

Cut out the outline of the shape, leaving a generous ⅛" fusible allowance outside the drawn line.

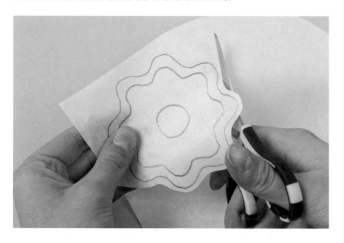

Cut across the drawn line of the outside flower.

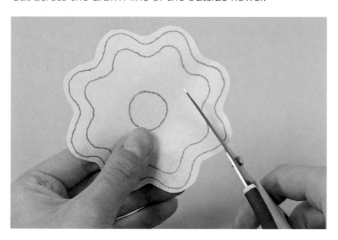

Cut away the center of the shape, leaving a generous ⅛" fusible allowance on the inside of the drawn line.

Cut the remaining shapes in the same manner.

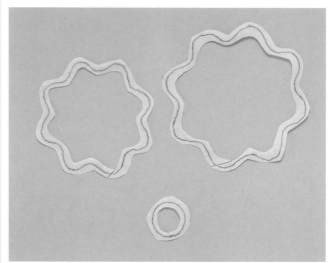

> **Tip**
> Never cut out the center of the shape by poking the center with scissors to make a hole and then cutting around the inside of the drawn line. The scissors poking the center will weaken the bond of the fusible web with the paper and will encourage the web to pull away from under the traced lines. To reach the center of a shape, always cut across the drawn line.

## Fusing Appliqué Pieces to Fabric

Set the iron setting between "wool" and "cotton," with no steam.

> **Note**
> Follow the fusible web manufacturer's directions carefully. If you under-iron the appliqué piece, it will not stick. You will know you haven't ironed long enough if the fusible sticks to the paper when you remove the paper. The fabric will also fray at the edges. The paper should come off smoothly. Iron a bit longer, taking care not to over-iron.
>
> Likewise, if you over-iron the appliqué piece, it also will not stick. Over-ironing causes the fusible to melt into plastic, which will not adhere to anything—which is how you will know that you've over-ironed. If this happens, you will need to cut new pieces of fusible.

Fuse the outline of the appliqué shape to the *wrong* side of your chosen fabrics.

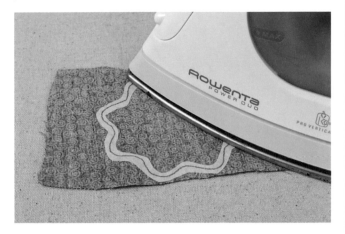

Allow the fabric to cool, and then cut out the appliqué shape on the drawn lines.

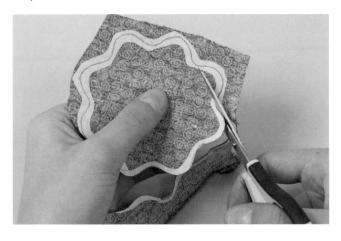

Now you have all the appliqué shapes ready for placement on the background fabric.

> **Tip** When I work on a project that has multiple elements, I fuse all the elements that belong on one particular fabric at the same time. This saves time. I then cut away the portion of fabric that has shapes fused to it. After fusing the shapes to all my fabrics, I cut them out all at the same time—usually while watching a movie or my favorite television show (since I *must* have something to occupy my hands). I find that if I do a tedious or time-consuming task while being enter-tained, the task doesn't seem quite so bad, and time passes quickly. It's multitasking at its best.

## Constructing the Appliqué Element

Use the template pattern as a reference for the placement of the flower pieces. Remove the fusible release paper to expose the fusible web on the flower center and the small piece of the flower. Leave the paper on the largest piece of the flower to keep it from being fused to the ironing board while you assemble the piece.

Arrange the flower pieces and fuse together.

Now remove the paper from the large piece of the flower and fuse the stacked flower onto the starched background. Fuse the leaf in place about ½" from the edge of the flower.

## Stitching the Appliqué

Refer to the stitch illustrations and instructions on pages 33–34 and 45 for stitch placement.

Carefully stitch around each piece. Pull the top thread to the back and knot the threads on the back as you finish stitching each element.

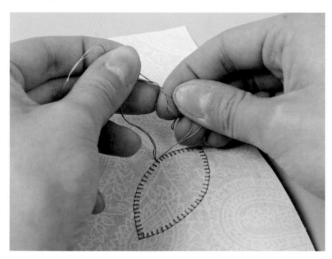

The piece will be slightly distorted when you finish stitching the complete block. Press the block right side down on the ironing board to flatten it. Pressing from the back will allow the design to come forward and not be flattened by the iron.

## Do We Have to Cut Away the Center of the Fusible?

I cut away the center of the fusible so my appliqué has the appearance of hand appliqué, giving that "fine" appearance to my work. If you leave the fusible under the entire surface of the fabric, the appliqué will be stiff to the hand and stiff in appearance. Leaving the fusible under the entire shape will also create a permanent, unattractive ridge in any piece that you fuse on top of a "join."

While this may be okay for crafty projects such as tea towels, children's clothing, sweatshirts, and so on, it's not appealing when you see it on a quilt. For quilt judges, it's a sign of how skilled the quiltmaker is. Taking the time to cut away the centers of the appliqué shapes is an indicator of the skill, expertise, and care that create a potentially award-winning quilt.

## How to "Fussy Place" Appliqué Shapes

The great thing about having the inside fusible removed from the appliqué piece is that it gives you a frame for finding a design in your fabric to showcase, just like we fussy cut designs for pieced quilts. Fussy placing a fusible shape lets you get just a hint of a different color or pattern on a petal, or dark at one tip and light at the other end of a leaf, or a printed flower in the middle of a shape.

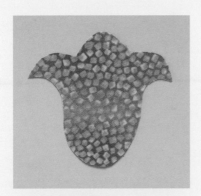

## When Is It Too Small or Too Tight to Cut Away the Center?

My rule is: anything ½" or under is too small to cut away the center—and, in the long run, it won't matter if the fusible is not cut away. I use a lot of little dots, sometimes as small as ¼" in diameter. I also use stems, tendrils, and other elements that may be only ½" in width.

## How to Deal with Tucked Elements on the Pattern and in the Design

I chose to present all the designs as whole elements rather than breaking up designs that contain features that are tucked under other pieces (see pages 10 and 112–124).

You'll find double dash marks, referred to as "tuck marks," on some of the pattern pieces to indicate that these sections of a piece will be tucked under other appliqué shapes. Transfer those marks to the fusible tracings so you know where they go when you are ready to build the block.

Along the edges with tuck marks, cut the fusible web on the traced line. Elsewhere, cut the fusible a generous ⅛" outside the line (see page 36). When you fuse that piece to the appliqué fabric, the tuck marks will remind you to add a ⅛" seam allowance of fabric to that section of the appliqué shape when you cut out the element. Then, when you fuse that element to the background, you will tuck under just fabric, not fabric *and* fusible.

## Preparing the Background Fabric and Centering the Appliqué

To start, always cut the piece of background fabric at least 1½" larger than it will be when it is finished. During the stitching process, the background will shrink and become a bit misshapen. Press on the wrong side and trim it to the proper size *after* all the appliqué work is finished.

Prepare the background fabric by starching it to the consistency of a piece of copy paper—not overly stiff. This will provide the stabilization that the block needs so it will not warp during the stitching process. You won't use any additional stabilizer notions for this method of machine appliqué. You may need to apply the starch more than once, in layers, to get it to the right stiffness. Reapply starch as needed during the stitching process if your background becomes limp.

Fold the background piece in half and fold it in half again, so you're quartering the fabric, and make a light finger crease along the folds of the block. Then center the pattern over the crease lines on the fabric.

## Stems and Vines: Fused or Bias?

Stems or vines will be the first layer of the appliqué design on the background fabric. Do you want the stems to be made out of bias strips, or do you want to trace them on fusible web? It's your choice.

## Fused Stems and Vines

Trace all the stem or vine pieces with their curvy shapes and fuse them in place on the background before layering other appliqué shapes to build the piece. Stitch these stems with a blanket stitch as you do the rest of the appliqué.

## Bias Stems and Vines

Bias stems are the traditional way of making stems for appliqué. I like using bias stems the best, as I feel that they make my appliqué look more thoughtfully complete. They take a little longer, but they finish nicely.

With your rotary cutter, ruler, and mat, cut bias strips of fabric. The bias is a 45° angle from the selvage edge of the fabric.

I like using a ⅞" (cut width) bias strip for most stems—it's not too thin or too thick.

Each project in this book will list how many inches of bias strips you need to cut for the stems.

You can either use a bias maker tool such as the one shown in Supplies (page 26) or follow my tri-fold method below.

### TRI-FOLD BIAS STRIPS

Use a steam iron for this technique. Use the weight and heat of the iron to get a nice flat fold on the strip.

At the ironing board, fold the bottom long edge of the strip up one-third of the width and press with the iron to make a creased fold. Press all the way along the strip.

Turn the strip so the fold is away from you.

Now fold the other edge up one-third to meet the first fold, just slightly before the fold so the raw edge will be under the strip when it is appliquéd.

Baste the bias strip closed with a hand-sewing needle and single strand of thread, using 1″-long stitches.

Now the bias stem is ready to use. It will bend easily into whatever shape you desire.

## Pattern Placement

I prefer to transfer only stem lines from the pattern to the background fabric. Then if other design elements need to be adjusted, lines that won't disappear are not left on the fabric. If you draw a placement line that you don't use and iron over it, the line is made permanent and will stay on the fabric. This happens often during the fusing process, as you continue to press the entire background piece as you fuse appliqué shapes and elements.

Transferring only the stem lines allows me to follow my original pattern by placing the flowers, leaves, and other design elements where I wish and to adjust them if necessary without worrying about lines that I couldn't follow or cover up. No need to trace the shape of every leaf and flower, just the stem! If there are no stems, simply create the pattern on the background free-form.

Make the placement lines for the stems by using either of the following methods:

- Place the pattern on a lightbox, and the fabric on top of the pattern. Trace the lines with a chalk pencil onto the starched background fabric.

- Trace the lines with a tracing stylus, with the pattern on top of the background fabric and Chacopy paper (see page 31) between the pattern and fabric.

## Adding the Bias Stems

Following the drawn lines, place the end of a stem at the beginning of a placement line and pin the stem in place, covering the line. Follow the shape of the line, laying down more stem and pinning it in place until you have covered the whole line with the stem. Clip off any extra stem and set it aside. The stems will stick up in places where the curves are tighter, but don't worry—you will press them flat after basting.

Thread a needle with a contrasting thread and baste the stem to the background using large stitches (1″ long). Baste along the center of the stem so the edges can be folded back for leaf placement.

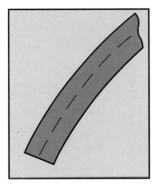

Baste with contrasting thread.

When all the stems are in place, remove the pins and lightly press the stems so they flatten into place.

## Adding the Rest of the Elements

Now you're ready to place, layer, and fuse the rest of the appliqué elements onto the background. I usually do this at the ironing board so I don't have to carry the pieces across the room.

Remove the release paper from each of the appliqué pieces to expose the fusible web. If the release paper isn't releasing easily, pinch the fused fabric to release the paper.

Arrange the appliqué pieces on the background fabric, taking care to tuck the edges of tucked pieces securely. Gently press the appliqué pieces in place, making sure that they don't move during pressing and that they are all firmly adhered.

When all the shapes are fused in place, you can begin to stitch around them.

Stitch all the other appliqué elements before stitching the bias stems, which will be the very last thing you stitch. You may have tucked the points of leaves underneath the stems, so you must stitch all the leaves first. The basting stitches that keep the stems in place will allow you to fold the stem back to stitch around each entire leaf.

To finally stitch the stems, switch to a straight stitch and stitch ¹⁄₁₆″ from each edge slowly, pivoting as necessary.

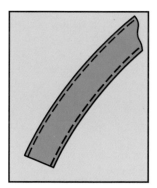

Stitch ¹⁄₁₆″ from edges.

Pull the thread tails to the back, tie them off, and bury them in the stem. Remove the basting stitches.

 **Note** I prefer to use a straight stitch along the edges of bias stems instead of a blanket stitch because I think it has a lighter appearance on the bias. The blanket stitch looks heavy.

Once the block is completely stitched, press and trim it to the required size. Be very careful not to trim it too small, as you may end up losing some of the appliqué in the seam allowance once the blocks are all sewn together.

# Stitching the Fused Appliqué Pieces

## Stitch Selection

There are several stitches that you can use to stitch around appliqué pieces. My favorite stitch is the *blanket stitch* because it frames the appliqué and adds a decorative touch to the fabrics. The stitches also help keep the fabrics firmly in place so there is no raveling in the future.

If your sewing machine doesn't have a blanket stitch, use a blind hem or zigzag stitch.

Your machine will generally have more than one blanket stitch. The ideal blanket stitch will stitch forward with one or two stitches and then zig and zag in place. Other blanket stitches will take a straight stitch, backstitch, and straight stitch before taking another straight stitch. This stitch is difficult to master around the curves and may produce a feathery look along the outside edge.

Some machines will perform the blanket stitch backward (from left to right, rather than right to left). You may be able to choose the mirror setting on your machine to switch the orientation, or you may need to stitch it backward. Either way, once you've practiced, your stitching will be smooth and beautiful.

The *blind hem* stitch is a utility stitch found on most sewing machines. It is several tiny straight stitches with a V-shaped zigzag. This stitch can be adjusted so it will be shorter and narrower and will close up the V to resemble the blanket stitch.

The *zigzag* is a fine alternative for machine appliqué if you don't have a blanket stitch on your machine. The zigzag needs to be set small for it to look neat.

Any straight areas of the appliqué designs will be stitched exactly as on your stitch sample—straight with no pivoting. However, on any part that is not straight, or is curvy, you will need to pivot.

You can practice stitching and correct stitch placement by making the appliqué sample set (page 35).

## Beginning and Ending the Stitching

Always start your stitching one-third of the way from the top point of a leaf, or in the curve of another shape. Never start at a point, where the join between the beginning and ending stitches will be most obvious.

If you usually have your sewing machine set to cut thread or knot off thread when you are finished stitching, you need to disable those settings for this type of stitching.

When you begin stitching, you must have thread tails. I usually hold onto them by wrapping them around my index finger as pictured.

This keeps the threads from bunching up on the back and creating a thread nest. It also reminds me to keep them out of the way so I don't stitch over them as I'm stitching around the appliqué shape.

Stitch around the entire shape, ending just before or at the first stitch.

Remove the appliqué from the sewing machine and snip the threads, leaving a good-length tail. Thread the tail into the top of a self-threading needle.

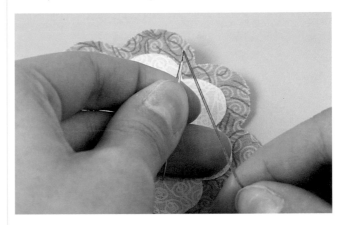

Insert the needle at the beginning stitch and bring the threads to the back of the piece.

Tie off the threads using a surgeon's knot (see Definitions, page 154) and clip threads close to the knot. Do not clip the knot.

## How to Stitch Curves

Pivoting is the one technique you will use most when stitching appliqué designs. It's essential that you learn the most important rule of pivoting: *always pivot in the background fabric*—never in the appliqué or while the stitch is in a zig step.

If you pivot in a zig step, the stitch will open up into a V or cross over itself.

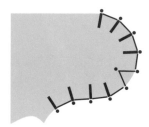

Dots represent pivot points.

On some curves, you need to pivot every second or third stitch. With very small circles, it may be necessary to pivot every stitch.

The needle must be in the down position when you pivot to keep the appliqué in place. You will raise the presser foot to pivot the edge of the appliqué into place so the next stitch will be made right along the edge of the appliqué—or so that the zig stitch will be perpendicular to the edge. Always make sure that you stop to pivot in the background fabric.

Stitching inside curves is exactly the same as stitching outside curves. You want the stitches to be perpendicular to the edge of the appliqué.

**Tip**

The stitches on a curve need to be perpendicular to the edge of the curve—like the spokes on a bicycle wheel. When stitching circles and curves, if you will imagine an X in the center of the piece, you can use it to line up the zig stitches so they are more uniform, rather than meandering in an unappealing way.

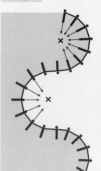

## Outside Points

Practice stitching outside points on a simple leaf shape.

Stitch along the outside curve until you're close to the point. Stop with the needle in the background and remember where you are in the stitch cycle—was the last stitch a zag or a straight stitch?

Take a stitch to get to the point without going beyond it. This may need to be done manually by lifting the presser foot and turning the machine wheel by hand to get into the right place at the point.

At the point, pivot the piece so you take a perpendicular stitch into the leaf—stitch a zig into the end of the point and zag back, and then pivot and continue stitching the leaf until you get to the next point and repeat.

It's extremely important for the points to be stitched down—otherwise they will curl up when the quilt is laundered or has been used. You want all the appliqué shapes to be securely stitched.

It will take some practice to get it perfect, but practice is good! The more I practice stitching, the better my stitching gets.

## Inside Points

Inside points are the opposite of outside points, but treat them and stitch them just the same—stopping at the point and taking a zig in perpendicular to the edge and a zag out to the background. You may need to adjust the needle placement to get in to the point. You will do this manually—just as you do when stitching an outside point.

# Stitch Stacked Elements before Fusing to the Background

 **Note** Do not starch any of the appliqué pieces—only the background!

If you stitch stacked elements, such as flowers, together before placing them on the background, you'll stitch a smaller, more compact piece that is easier to work with. Begin with the center design and stitch around it, changing thread colors as necessary to stitch the rest of the piece. Refrain from stitching the outer edge of the piece.

After the insides are stitched, remove the release paper from the bottom of the stack and fuse the stitched stacked elements in place on the background; then stitch around the outer edge.

## Knee-Lift vs. Lifting the Presser Foot by Hand

I learned this method by lifting the presser foot by hand to pivot my stitches, and therefore rest my right hand on the machine bed. My sewing machine has a knee-lift attachment that I have never used. (And I haven't learned how to be comfortable using it.) If you usually use a knee-lift to lift your presser foot, use it here as well!

# Hand Appliqué

There is only one method of hand appliqué that I can wholeheartedly recommend, and that is the one that my friend Holly Mabutas of Eat Cake Graphics developed and taught me. I am still no good at needle-turn appliqué, but Holly's method allows me to achieve a finished hand appliqué that most closely resembles needle-turn. You will be amazed at how beautifully this hand appliqué turns out.

Assemble the supplies as noted on pages 26–32.

For practice, use the Simple Shapes—Flower and Leaf patterns on page 35.

Trace the pattern pieces individually onto the *dull side* of freezer paper. Use a double dash to indicate tuck marks for any tucked elements.

Cut out the pieces *on the solid line.*

Iron the cut-out freezer-paper pieces to the fabric. Freezer-paper pieces should be *shiny side down*, while the fabric should be *right side up.* Leave about ½" between all the pieces. Make sure the freezer-paper pieces are secure!

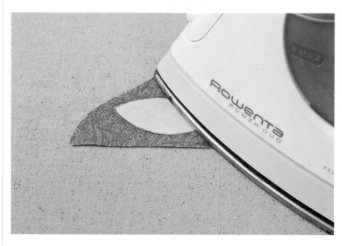

> **Tip** Place a piece of leftover cardboard under the appliqué fabrics when you press the freezer paper to the fabric. It will help make a better bond so the freezer paper doesn't peel away while you're working on the rest of the steps.

Cut out the fabric pieces, leaving a scant ¼" seam allowance around the freezer-paper shape. Leave only ⅛" at the tuck marks.

Clip the inside curves. Don't clip too far in or past the freezer paper.

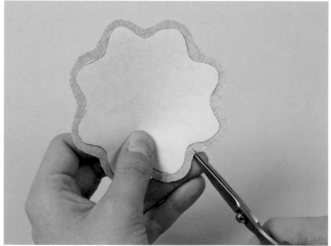

You can clip the tips off points, but be sure to leave a little bit of fabric above the freezer-paper piece.

Once I cut out all the pieces, I usually press them with the iron one more time before gluing. This resecures any parts of the freezer paper, especially tips or small pieces, that might have come loose.

Apply glue (from a gluestick) to the scant ¼" seam allowance on the wrong side of the fabric. Make swipes of glue from the inside toward the outside edge. You can glue in sections or, for small pieces, glue all the way around at once. Do not apply glue to areas with tuck marks.

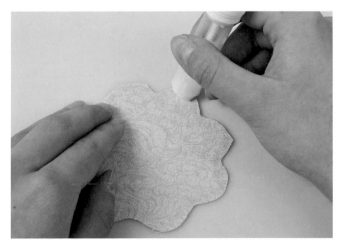

Use a sponge to wipe off the gluestick when it gets "thready." I also cap my gluestick after each piece.

Working from the wrong side of the fabric (where you just glued), turn the fabric edge back on itself so that it sticks to the glue. What you're "feeling" for is the tension between the fabric and the edge of the freezer paper to know you've

turned back just enough of the fabric. Continue doing this until the shape is completely turned. However, do not turn back areas with tuck marks. The ⅛" fabric allowance will be tucked under another piece.

Once the edges are turned, you can pull off the freezer paper or leave it on until all the pieces are finished.

After you pull the freezer paper off, give the piece or pieces a quick tap with the iron.

A flat piece is a good piece.

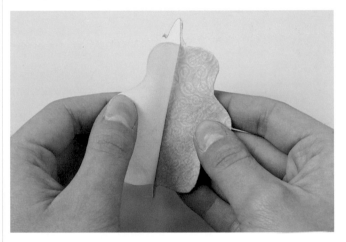

Once all the pieces are prepared, place the pattern on top of a disposable kitchen mat, and then place a see-through sheet protector on top of the pattern. Start placing the finished pieces on top of the sheet protector, following the outline of the pattern.

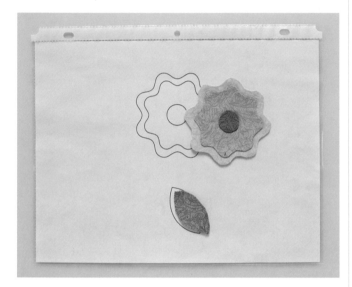

Sometimes I use tweezers to hold small pieces. It's easier to place them, and the tweezers keep the glue off your fingers.

Place little dots of appliqué glue along the back edge of the flower center and place it on top of the small piece of the flower. Place dots of glue on the back edge of the small piece of the flower and place it on the top of the large piece of the flower.

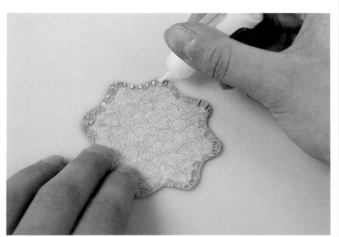

Position the leaf next to the edge of the stacked flower. If you prefer to have the leaf under the edge of the flower, place dots of glue on the top fabric edge of the leaf that will go under the flower before positioning the leaf.

Now the pieces are ready to stitch!

Thread an appliqué needle with a 24″ strand of silk thread.

Place the prepared pieces on the background fabric. Using a blind stitch, take ⅛″ stitches along the edge of the leaf, coming up from the back side of the appliqué and inserting the needle back into the background where the needle came up.

If there are any sharp points along the edge of the appliqué where it should be smoothly curved, you can adjust the edge in the stitching stage.

Stitch the flower. Begin with the large piece of the flower, and then stitch the smaller pieces, going through all the layers of fabric.

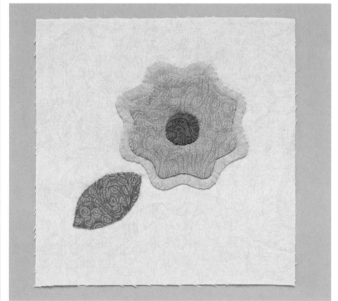

You'll get the hang of it quickly and enjoy this method as much as I do.

The best things about Holly's method of hand appliqué:

**No pins!** Everything is put together using glue, so you'll never lose another pin in the sofa or on the floor (although I can't say the same for your needle).

**It's portable!** Just pick up the finished units and try them on different background fabrics.

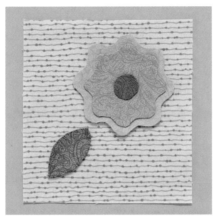
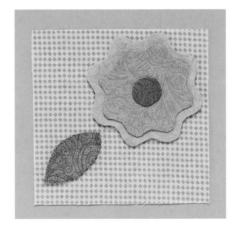

You can also take supplies and prepared pieces with you in a re-sealable plastic zipper bag or a fancy tote.

Holly says, "New techniques have learning curves, just like everything else that's new. Don't be too hard on yourself if things aren't perfect the first time or even the second. With a little patience and practice, you'll do just fine."

# CHAPTER 6

# The Basics of Design for Blocks and Quilts

*Do not fear mistakes. There are none.* —Miles Davis

> ### Design *noun*
>
> **1.** the way in which something is planned and made
> **2.** a drawing or other graphical representation of something that shows how it is to be made
> **3.** a pattern or shape, sometimes repeated, used for decoration
> **4.** the process and techniques of designing things
> **5.** a plan or scheme for something
> **6.** something that is planned or intended

*Design.* Does that word make you want to run in the other direction with fear? Or does it excite you with possibilities? Before I began designing my own quilts, I lived with the fear that I was a better re-creator than a creator. As time went on and I climbed out on that limb, I realized that designing is nothing more than putting the ideas floating around in my head down on paper.

## What If the Design Isn't Right?

Do you remember being in kindergarten and looking forward to painting time? That was the highlight of the day. Even better if it was finger painting rather than painting with a brush—the messier the better.

A researcher performed a study with elementary school children to determine how creative they were and at what age the desire to create begins to wane. The researcher asked the children who considered themselves to be artists. All the kindergartners raised their hands. By the third grade, only a few raised their hands. By the sixth grade, no hands were raised, and the students looked around to see who would raise their hands for something so childish.

Let go of this fear—or reticence—of trying to design something that is uniquely yours. Let yourself go!

Besides, just like our kindergarten paintings that were taped to the refrigerator and then eventually tossed out, it's just paper—either file it for future refining or toss it.

## Begin with Simple Tools and Shapes

### Tools

I like to use tools that are inexpensive and easy to find.

- **A roll of white paper**    I get a large roll of butcher paper from a discount warehouse store or a small roll of easel paper from Ikea. The paper from the warehouse store is a big fat roll that is 18″ wide and will last forever; the paper from Ikea is a skinny roll 18½″ wide.

- **A roll of artist "trash" paper**    You can find this at artist supply stores. It's a roll of tracing paper that comes in varying widths. One roll will last you a long time. I like to use this paper to adapt and refine my designs from the originals drawn on the white paper.

- **Ticonderoga Tri-Write Pencils**    These are three-sided 2/HB soft lead pencils. I keep a battery-operated pencil sharpener handy for these.

- **Design kneaded eraser**    You will want a soft artist's eraser that won't tear your paper; this is available at artist supply stores.

- **Blue painter's tape**   The blue tape is low-tack, so it comes up easily and doesn't tear your paper or remove the finish from your work surface. For more uses, see Basic Supplies (page 30).

- **Ruler**   I usually just grab whichever quilting ruler is handy. I also love using a flexible ruler for those curves that I just can't make freehand.

- **A black permanent fine-tip marking pen**   A Micron Pigma pen, an ultra-fine-line Sharpie, or a Copic marker are all good choices—and all can be found at artist supply or office supply stores. Once I have my design just the way I want it, I draw over all the lines with the permanent marker and erase all the pencil lines.

## Shapes

The easiest way to begin designing is to realize how basic the shapes of appliqué design really are—and that there are only a few.

The X

The diamond

The O

The U

 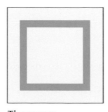

The square

The cross

The triangle

The V

# Balance

Think of the scales that Lady Justice holds—they represent balance. If you put too many items on one side, the scale tips. You want your creation to form a satisfying and harmonious design, with nothing out of proportion. You may need to make a flower larger or a leaf smaller or add more leaves in an area, but you have to play with the balance. Just like we want to make sure the blocks are laid out in a balanced way, so the quilt isn't too top-heavy with one color or technique, we want to make sure the design isn't too heavy in one area and too sparse in another.

A great way to check your work is to pin it on your design wall and stand back to view it.

Another key to balance is knowing that an odd number of items is more interesting than an even number—so three flowers will be more appealing than four flowers. If you follow the design shapes outlined and pictured above, your balance will be perfect.

# Designing Your Block

Think of the background as a canvas. Begin with a piece of tracing paper that is 2″ larger than the finished block. Appliqué blocks can be any size you wish. I have made appliqué blocks ranging from 4″ up to 18″, and it's just as easy to design an 18″ block as it is a 4″ block. The only difference is that you will put more design elements in larger blocks.

If your paper is too small for the pattern that you want to make, it's okay to tape pieces of paper together to get the right size.

Use the Catalog of Appliqué Design Elements in Chapter 12 (page 105) to choose which designs to add to your pattern.

Will you begin with a vase and fill it with flowers?

Did you fall in love with one particular flower that you want to base your pattern on?

Do you like the O shape better than the X?

Will you use a variety of leaves or use leaves sparingly so you can add a dragonfly or a bird?

Will you use a bias vine as the main shape and fill in the design with elements, or will you create your design with an invisible main shape?

Decide which shape you would like to use and lightly draw it on the paper. It will be a placeholder for the design, which you will refine as you add the design elements.

After you choose the shape, place your drawn design shape over each of the design elements you want to add to the pattern and trace them into position.

When you are satisfied with the design of the pattern, use it for placement on the background fabric. Trace the design elements onto sheets of fusible web and prepare the appliqué for your new block (pages 35–38).

# When Less Is More

When designing, don't try to fill up every available space of the background.

Designs need to be balanced, with just enough appliqué elements, and should not be too crowded. If your pattern is too crowded, it will not allow the eye to rest and take in the whole design—it will look chaotic. Remember that each design element you put into the pattern must be prepared and stitched.

You can see in the block sketches to the left that one is overcrowded with too many elements; the other is balanced just right.

In her book *Baltimore Elegance*, Elly Sienkiewicz made a special note on the subject of airiness. She said, "Airiness is a common element of classic Album quilts. For example, lots of background fabric appears behind the appliqués. ... Flowers are lifted so that light (background) moves around and between them. It is fun to look at such blocks in the fanciest old Baltimores and see that there are usually unrealistically few (or no) stems descending from a lush cluster of flowers. ... Certain Album blocks excel at realism, but it seems that airiness trumps realism. After so long in the company of these old Albums, you might think the quilters sometimes tried to show unseen things, such as a breeze, a beam of sunlight, or the unseen hand of God."

To me, "airiness" equates to "less is more."

# Don't Forget to Leave Room for the Quilting

Airiness is important not only to the design itself, but also in terms of leaving room for quilting. If you fill up all the available space, how will you be able to grace your quilt with beautiful quilting designs?

If you design your quilt with the quilting in mind, you will enable the appliqué to be beautifully simple while allowing room for quilting motifs such as feathers, tendrils, crosshatching, or other designs that are essential for the completion of the quilt.

Quilting is such an essential part of the quilt. If you don't purposefully leave open areas when designing, you'll have room only to mirror the appliqué.

You can even add preliminary quilting designs to your pattern—in pencil, just in case you change your mind later. It's a great way to view the entire project and solidify it in your mind.

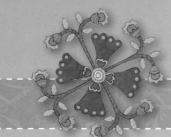

# CHAPTER 7

# Designing Your Quilt

*A design isn't finished until somebody is using it.—Brenda Laurel*

> ## Quilt   *noun, verb*
>
> **1.** a bed cover made of two layers of fabric stitched together, with interior padding of cotton or feathers held in place by decorative intersecting seams
> **2.** something that resembles a quilt or is quilted
> **3.** to make a fabric article, especially a bed cover, by sewing two layers of fabric together with a filling, especially using decorative stitching

## Size Matters

While we know that making a quilt involves much more than simply sewing two layers of fabric together with batting in between, the fundamentals of quilt design are universally the same. We start the quilt top by determining what size we want our quilt to be.

Here is a list of size issues to consider before beginning your quilt design:

- How will you use your quilt?

    Is it meant to be art, or will it be a utilitarian quilt?

- Will it be a wallhanging, or will you use it on a bed?

    A wallhanging will be smaller.

    A bed quilt will need to be designed with the mattress size, side drop, and optional pillow tuck in mind.

- Are you using fabrics that you have only a little left of and that you can't find any more of?

    For example, if you have only three yards of background fabric, your quilt can only be that big—blocks and border included—unless you use two backgrounds, such as in *Greenhouse* (page 82).

    If you have a nice assortment of fabrics for appliqué, but you just ran out of the one you like the most, add another fabric that will be complementary to the quilt's palette.

- Do you want to use a solid black background, but you can't find any more of that particular dye lot and you don't have enough for the whole quilt?

    Either design your quilt to fit the size of the fabric you have available or purchase a new black solid. One solution is to purchase a black solid that is consistently dyed so that all the bolts are the same no matter where or when you buy them, such as Michael Miller Jet Black or Robert Kaufman Jet Black.

# Will You Enter Your Quilt into Competition?

Yes, you have to know now.

If you begin your quilt with the goal of entering it into competition, any competition, you will plan to do your very best work on it. It doesn't matter what type of competitive show you want to enter—the county or state fair, your guild's quilt show, or a national quilt show. There are deadlines to consider for each show, and you need to make sure that you're allotting yourself the proper amount of time to complete and photograph your potential entry.

Believe it or not, even though you may have sworn that your work isn't worthy to be in a show, the time will come when someone will see your quilt and insist that you enter it into a show. The results may amaze you!

## Design with the Quilting in Mind

As mentioned in the previous chapter, you need to design your whole quilt with the quilting in mind—whether you do your own quilting or send it to a professional quilter.

You will want to think about whether you want it to be quilted with a computerized design or free motion, or with straight crosshatching lines. As you make the quilt, you may start to see quilting designs emerge around your beautiful appliqué.

## How to Begin

Do you begin with one block and then build from there?

Do you begin with a center motif?

Do you begin with an idea for a beautiful border and then build the inside?

The answer to all three of these questions is yes.

You can begin at any of these points—from one element, from the center of the quilt and work out, or from the outside border and work in.

You need to begin with an idea and see where the design takes you. That's how I design every time—beginning in one place and then building on the rest as I go.

The only time I have "seen" a whole quilt design is when I designed *Pickle Road Garden.* I saw the quilt in my mind when I was visiting at Mark Lipinski's house right after he had received 30 bolts of Katmandu fabric. He laid them out on the dining room table—that wonderful riot of patterns and color—and I *knew* how they would look on a solid black background. I envisioned the pieced block and the swirly appliqué because I had seen them as artwork in an issue of *Quilter's Home* magazine. What a perfect marriage of art design and Mark's fabric that quilt (page 71) is!

# The Quilt Will Tell You When It's Complete

Just like your quilt will tell you what it wants during the design and construction phases, your appliqué quilt will tell you when it's complete. Until then, it's not done.

You've designed a gorgeous quilt and finished all the appliqué work, and now it's hanging on the design wall. You're pleased with your work, and you leave it up for a couple of days so you can look at it and make sure it's right. You walk by it and suddenly you stop and realize that something is missing. How could that be? You check your patterns and, yes, all the designs are there—but something is still missing.

There is a little detail here or there that, the quilt is telling you, would make the difference between a gorgeous quilt and a truly amazing quilt. You can turn your back and pronounce it finished, but you know the quilt will tell you, long after it's quilted and bound, that you should have attended to that little detail.

This happened to me when I was designing *Midnight in the Garden*.

I thought I was finished when I had the center motif and all the borders laid out. I was so happy, and I went to bed for the night. When I got up the next morning, I looked at it and thought, "Hmm, something's not quite right. ..." I checked every detail to make sure I hadn't missed a shape or used the wrong fabric in one piece. Everything was there, but suddenly I was aware of a tiny little detail that would make this quilt *amazing*. And don't we all want amazing quilts? It was adding the little yellow dots in the borders, which act like asterisks and underscore the center flowers in the border—and *they had to be there.* I groaned because they are the most labor-intensive things to stitch, but so worth it. I knew when they were all in place that the quilt was then finished.

Since then, those little dots have almost become a signature design in my appliqué.

Compare this quilt in progress to the finished quilt on page 79. I think you'll agree that the yellow dots on the finished quilt add some nice interest.

# CHAPTER 8

# Quilt Gallery

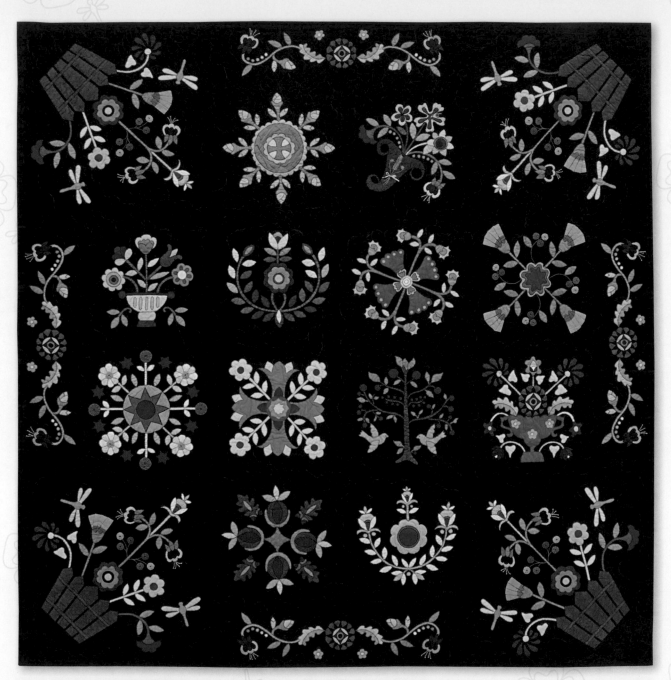

***West of Baltimore,*** Aneda Phillips, Campbell, California, 2006, 82" × 82".
Machine quilting by Melodee Wade, Sunnyvale, California.

The West of Baltimore quilt was designed as a block of the month for students who wanted to continue taking classes from me as a group. I would design one block, teach it to them, and then have the next block designed by the next month. The blocks became progressively more challenging as the months went on. Aneda designed her quilt's layout, inspired by a quilt from Barbara Brackman's book *Prairie Flower: A Year on the Plains.*
I loved Aneda's quilt as soon as I saw it and knew that it needed to be the cover for my pattern. It was featured in the *Keepsake Quilting* catalog for two years.

***It Happens Every Spring,*** Annie Smith, San Jose, California, 1989–2002, 64" × 82".
Machine quilting by Melodee Wade, Sunnyvale, California.

How do baseball and Laura Ashley work together? In this quilt, I used a patchwork kit purchased at a Laura Ashley store and worked on the hand appliquéd hearts at my two oldest kids' Little League baseball games beginning in 1989. I put the pieces away for a decade and then found them in a box in 2001. My youngest was playing Little League by then, and I hauled them out and finished the hand appliqué at his games. The quilt was finally finished and named after that old Ray Milland movie about baseball, my favorite sport.

*Let Your Light So Shine*, designed by Annie Smith, San Jose, California, 2001. Hand appliqué, machine appliqué, and machine piecing by Sharon Smith, Lisa Wallace, Molly Hauptman, Tina Davis, Anita Hawkins, Mary Lou Schar, Rose Adams, Melanie Merrill Fields, June Ellington, and Annie Smith. Machine quilting by Melodee Wade, Sunnyvale, California. Photo by Martin Nohr.

We made this group quilt for our dear friend Rae Ann Merrill at the end of her calling as our church women's leader. During her years of service, Rae Ann was responsible for over 250 families and their physical, social, and emotional needs. Rae Ann is a wonderful quilter, and we knew she would love this quilt, which is a symbolic memento of her friends and the women she served. The outside vines are the traced hands of the women of the church, reduced 50 percent for the patterns, creating "flowers" in Rae Ann's garden.

*50th Wedding Anniversary Quilt*, Annie Smith, San Jose, California, 2005. Machine appliqué. Machine quilting by Melodee Wade, Sunnyvale, California. Quilt commissioned by the children of Ray and Ann Wood. Photo by author.

This special quilt incorporated family photos with pieced designs and appliqué symbolic of the Wood family. The stars are Ray and Ann's children, the hearts are grandchildren, and the apples at the base of the tree are for the great-grandchildren that will continue the family pedigree.

*Gran's Memory Quilt* border, Annie Smith, Pacific Grove, California, 2002, 14" × 36"

I designed this border in Sue Nickels's class at the second Empty Spools Seminar that I attended. It is to be a part of a memory quilt of my maternal grandmother, with all the elements symbolic of my time spent at her home on a cherry orchard. It is one of my favorite designs, and one day I will design the rest of the quilt!

*What a Girl Wants,* Annie Smith, San Jose, California, 2002, 52" × 52". Machine appliqué.
Machine quilting by Melodee Wade, Sunnyvale, California.

Hearts, chocolates, and roses: what more could a girl want? This quilt was inspired by the strawberry
and chocolate batik fabric.

*West of Baltimore* prototype blocks, Annie Smith, 2004

The prairie rose, carnation, and chrysanthemum were all inspired by antique appliqué blocks.

*Urban Garden*, Valerie Burton, Kaysville, Utah, 2008, 54" × 54"

Valerie created *Urban Garden* from the first fabric line that her neighbor, Rachel Brenchley, designed for Moda—Urban Couture by Basic Grey. She designed this quilt to feature the fabric in Moda's booth at Quilt Market. There were so many gold fabrics in the collection that Valerie kept thinking of sunflowers. The 3-D pieced pinwheels have become Valerie's signature design.

*Rockets and Robots,* Annie Smith, San Jose, California, 2007, 66″ × 53″.
Machine appliqué. Machine quilting by Shelley Nealon of Quilted Bliss, Campbell, California.

Needing a new pattern design for Quilt Market, I decided to pay homage to my husband's childhood collection of wind-up metal robots and his love of everything NASA. We watched the entire *Star Trek: Voyager* series while I worked on this quilt. The rockets are embellished with colored Swarovski crystals for lights. The crystals also make the details on the robots crackle with fire.

*All Hearts Come Home for Christmas*, Annie Smith, San Jose, California, 2003.
Machine piecing, paper piecing, and machine appliqué. Machine quilting by Melodee Wade, Sunnyvale, California. Photo by author.

*All Hearts* was made for my son, who spent two years away from home in northern Italy performing missionary service. We missed two Christmases with him, and he was coming home just in time for Christmas 2003. The design of this quilt is symbolic of his mission, our family, and his future family—even though it is a Christmas quilt. This quilt was my first published pattern.

*Mom's Apron Strings*, Annie Smith, San Jose, California, 2007, 40" × 40".
Machine appliqué, machine construction, and hand embroidery. Machine quilting by Melodee Wade, Sunnyvale, California.

My mom passed away suddenly in 2005 and left us 30 years of a household to sort and divide. Somehow, I got all my mom's aprons and her sewing kit. In an attempt to make a passage quilt with her belongings, I got the idea for this quilt. Using a printed hankie, I embroidered "My heart is tied with my Mother's apron strings" and created replicas of my mom's aprons for the quilt.

*A Rose Tree in a Baltimore Garden* coat,
Annie Smith, Morgan Hill, California, 2008.

A companion piece for the *Midnight in the Garden*
quilt (project on page 79), the shawl collar of the
coat has a traditional rose tree design that wraps
around to the front of the coat. The princess-
seam coat is a commercial pattern. Fabric panels
were free-motion quilted by Melodee Wade. Coat
pieces were cut out of the panels, and appliqué
designs were created and carried over to adjacent
pieces as they were joined to assemble the entire
coat. The color palette was inspired by a Robert
Kaufman fabric, Florentine by Peggy Toole, which
was used as the coat's lining.

***Everyday Coat,*** Annie Smith, Pacific Grove and Morgan Hill, California, 2009. Machine appliqué. Machine quilting by Shelley Nealon of Quilted Bliss, Campbell, California.

Since I can't wear my Baltimore coat (page 67) around (it's like an evening gown), I thought I would make a coat that I could wear "every day." Using the same commercial pattern as the Baltimore coat, I changed the design and used beautiful Japanese import fabrics for the appliqué. I designed new appliqué elements—and used robin birds for the upper arms, to carry my son, Robin, around with me.

"Robin" sleeve detail

Compare the back design with the border on page 61.

*Flora Bella*, Annie Smith, San Jose, California, 2006, 58" × 82".
Machine appliqué and free-motion embellishment. Machine quilting by Melodee Wade, Sunnyvale, California.

After designing *West of Baltimore* as a block of the month, I heard many quilters admire the quilt while remarking, "Oh, I could never make that quilt. It's too big, and there is just too much detail." So I decided to design a quilt that was a little less labor-intensive, yet with a unique style.

I wanted the border edge treatment to be more than scalloped, so I designed a sculptured border that would reflect the flavor of the appliqué design.

*Quilter's Palette: Out of the Comfort Zone*, Annie Smith, San Jose, California, 2004, 52½″ × 52½″.
Machine piecing, paper-piecing, machine appliqué. Machine quilted by Melodee Wade, Sunnyvale, California.

The Quilter's Palette is another class that I created for a group of students who wanted to learn more quilting skills.
The quilt is a sampler of techniques, incorporating three ways to do machine appliqué, five ways to paper-piece a block,
and advanced quilting techniques. This quilt is unique: It has no borders, and when the blocks are put together with
the sashing, it is ready to quilt. I love the layered look of the curved edges of the quilt, making it appear that there is a
quilt on top of another quilt. The center (Thistle Flower) and Butterfly blocks are my original design.
*Quilter's Palette* is a good example of adding appliquéd blocks and interest to a pieced quilt, as outlined in Chapter 11
(page 104). I love mixing pieced quilt blocks and appliqué! In more recent versions of this teaching quilt, I've added
different blocks and much more appliqué. (The Carnival Ride block used in the quilt is an original design by
Judy Martin, 1990, from her book, *Scraps, Blocks & Quilts*. It is used with permission.)

# CHAPTER 9

# Three Appliqué Projects to Get You Started

Although this is a resource book that allows you to pick and choose your own appliqué elements, I offer you three projects to get you started—a sampling of sorts. The first is a traditionally sized block with three little companion blocks. The second is a small quilt, and the third is a multiple-block quilt.

The projects will help you get the hang of machine appliqué and how elements are put together. Read all the instructions before beginning a project. Use a highlighter to note any instructions that need special attention.

 **Note** I cut sashing and borders on the lengthwise grain of the fabric (parallel to the selvage). This provides more stability to the quilt and for the appliqué because there is no ease in the lengthwise grain. The yardage in the projects is sufficient for this.

## HOW TO USE THE PATTERNS

**Tip** To use any of the patterns in this book, trace a full-size pattern of your own to work from. Trace with a pencil, not a permanent pen, so the tracing doesn't bleed through onto the page. When you have finished tracing the full-size pattern, draw over the traced pencil lines with a permanent pen.

For large symmetrical designs, only half the pattern is given. Large asymmetrical patterns are divided in half, and both halves are provided.

To create a full pattern from a half pattern, start with a piece of tracing paper that is larger than the full-size pattern. Fold the paper in half, open it, and place the open sheet on the page with the crease from the fold lined up on the dashed line. Tape the paper in place with blue painter's tape so the paper doesn't slip during tracing. Trace the first half of the pattern completely.

*Tracing the second half of a symmetrical pattern:* Flip the tracing paper over to the back of the blank half and realign the fold on the dashed line, making sure that you also connect the traced lines so the design will align correctly. Trace the first half of the pattern again. You will have one tracing on the front of the tracing paper and one on the back of the tracing paper. When you open the paper flat, because the tracing paper is translucent, you'll be able to see the entire design. If you wish, draw over the traced pencil lines with a permanent pen so all of the traced lines will be on the same side.

*Tracing the second half of an asymmetrical pattern:* After tracing half of the pattern, align the fold and tracing lines with the other half of the pattern. Trace the second half to complete the pattern.

# FOUR BLOCKS SUITABLE FOR FRAMING

## Jacobean Tulips

The first project has simple motifs with basic shapes to get you warmed up. These can be made as blocks for a larger quilt, finished to use as wallhangings, or framed just like the samples.

The Jacobean Tulips block has traditional elements: a circular stem, leaves, stylized flowers, and small detailing. Use a 15″ × 15″ square of tracing paper to trace the full design.

The bird has 3 parts: a body and 2 wings. It is also carrying a small flower in its beak—which you may add or leave off. The stem and little ribbon detail are stitched using free-motion embroidery (see Chapter 11: Options for Appliqué Elements and Embellishments, page 104).

The rosebuds have several elements: bias stems, leaves, and 3-piece rosebuds. In addition, the tip of each rosebud has a ¼″ dot.

The dragonflies each have 5 parts: 1 body and 2-part wings on each side of the body.

Refer to Chapter 5: Appliqué Methods (page 33) for instruction on how to create the appliqué shapes, prepare bias strips, and use my method of machine appliqué.

*Jacobean Tulips*, by Annie Smith, Morgan Hill, California

**Finished block:** 15½″ × 15½″  |  **Framed block:** 20″ × 20″

## Materials

*Refer to the list on page 26 for basic supplies.*

- Paper-backed fusible web, 37″ wide: ½ yard (This yardage will be sufficient for all 4 blocks.)

- Background fabric: 1 fat quarter or ⅝ yard neutral print

- 4 green prints—dark for stems; medium dark, medium, and medium light for leaves: ¼ yard of each

- 5 rusty red prints in a gradation from dark red to medium pink for tulips: ¼ yard of each

*Materials continued on next page.*

- 2 gold prints—light and medium gold for circles and flower accents: scrap of each
- Batting fabric: 20″ × 20″ piece
- Backing fabric: 20″ × 20″ piece
- Binding fabric: ½ yard (This yardage will be sufficient for all 4 blocks.)

*Optional:*

- Picture frames: 1 frame 20″ × 20″ and 1 frame 20″ × 8″
- Light print fabric—foundation matting to display the blocks on: ¾ yard

## Cutting and Fusing Instructions

*Half of the symmetrical Jacobean Tulips pattern is on pattern pullout page P1 at the back of the book.*

1. Cut 1 square 18″ × 18″ for the background of the block.

2. From the dark green fabric, cut ⅞″-wide bias strips to total 28″ and prepare the stems. (Refer to Bias Stems and Vines and Tri-fold Bias Strips on pages 40–42.)

3. Transfer the stem placement lines onto the background. Do not transfer any other designs to the background.

4. Hand baste the stems to the background over the placement lines. Cut the stems to fit the placement lines after they have been basted to the background. Use the leftover stem pieces for the shorter stems.

5. Trace 29 large leaves, 6 medium-size leaves, and 3 small leaves.

6. Fuse 9 of the large leaf shapes to each of the medium-dark, medium, and medium-light green prints (27 altogether).

7. Fuse the 2 leftover large leaves to the medium green print and the 3 small leaves to the medium-light green print. The 3 small leaves will be placed at the top of the small tulip.

8. Fuse the 6 medium leaves to the dark red print. These leaves will be placed at the top of the large tulips.

9. Trace 1 small calyx and 2 large calyxes.

10. Fuse the calyxes to the medium-dark green print.

11. Trace each of the flower elements: 1 small tulip, 2 large tulips, and 1 complete center flower. (Refer to pages 35–40 for tracing instructions for tucked flowers and stacked flowers.)

12. Fuse the tulip and center flower shapes to the light-to-dark red prints and medium and light gold prints, following the fabric placement in the project photo on page 73.

13. Trace 1 large dot, 8 medium dots, and 4 small dots.

14. Fuse the large dot and 4 of the medium dots to the medium gold, and the remaining 4 medium dots and the 4 small dots to the light gold print.

15. Arrange and fuse the appliqué shapes on the background fabric. Stitch around each of the shapes with matching thread. Stitch the stems with a straight stitch ¹⁄₁₆″ from the edge.

 **Tip** Remember when choosing fabric for the flowers to follow the rules of nature. The stems are in shadow (darker), and the top leaves are in the sun (lighter). The base or inside of the flower is in shadow (darker), and the top or outside petals are in the sun (lighter).

## Finishing

After the block is stitched and quilted with a simple straight crosshatching design in the background, complete the block as follows:

1. Press and trim the block to 15½″ × 15½″.

2. Bind the block with a 2⅝″ (cut width) double-fold bias binding, using a ⅜″ seam allowance to sew the binding to the front of the block.

3. Hand stitch the binding to the back of the block.

4. Display or frame, as desired.

# Three Mini-quilts: A Bird, Rosebuds, and Dragonflies

Three mini-quilts: *A Bird*, *Rosebuds*, and *Dragonflies*, by Annie Smith, Morgan Hill, California

## Materials

*Refer to the list on page 26 for basic supplies.*

- Background fabric: 3 squares 6½″ × 6½″ of 3 different neutral prints for backgrounds

- Dark blue, medium blue, and medium-light blue prints: scraps for bird body and wings and dragonfly body

- Different blue print: scrap for dragonfly wings

- Light-to-dark reds prints and medium-light and medium-dark green prints left over from *Jacobean Tulips*: scraps for tiny heart-shaped flower, rosebuds, leaves, and bias stems

- Light gold print left over from *Jacobean Tulips*: scrap for ¼″ circles for rosebuds

- Batting: 3 pieces 8″ × 8″ each

- Backing: 3 pieces 8″ × 8″ each

**Finished blocks:** 5½″ × 5½″ each | **3 framed blocks:** 20″ × 8″

## Cutting and Fusing Instructions

*Turn to page 74 for instructions on laying out the block, the layering sequence, and stitching hints.*

### Bird

1. Choose a 6½″ × 6½″ square of neutral print for the background.

2. Trace 1 of each shape: body, right wing, left wing, and heart-shaped flower parts.

3. Fuse the body to the dark blue print.

4. Fuse 1 wing each to 2 different medium blue prints.

5. Fuse the flower parts to medium-light green and dark red.

6. Arrange and fuse the appliqué shapes on the background. Stitch around each of the shapes with matching thread.

After the bird is stitched, turn to Chapter 11: Options for Appliqué Elements and Embellishments (page 104), for free-motion embroidery instructions and hints, which you will use for the flower stem and ribbon before quilting the block.

# Rosebuds

1. Choose a 6½″ × 6½″ square of neutral print for the background.

2. From the medium-dark green print, cut ⅞″-wide bias strips to total 8″ and prepare the stems. (Refer to Bias Stems and Vines and Tri-fold Bias Strips on page 40.)

3. Transfer the stem placement lines onto the background. Do not transfer any other designs to the background.

4. Hand baste the stems to the background over the placement lines.

5. Trace 2 leaves, 3 small dots, and the shapes for 3 complete rosebuds.

6. Fuse the leaf shapes to the medium-light green print.

7. Fuse the rosebud shapes to the red prints, following the fabric placement in the photo above.

8. Fuse the 3 dots to the light gold print.

9. Arrange and fuse the appliqué shapes on the background. Stitch around each of the shapes with matching thread. Stitch the stems with a straight stitch ⅟₁₆″ from the edge. Turn under and press the raw edge at the stem tip before stitching.

# Dragonflies

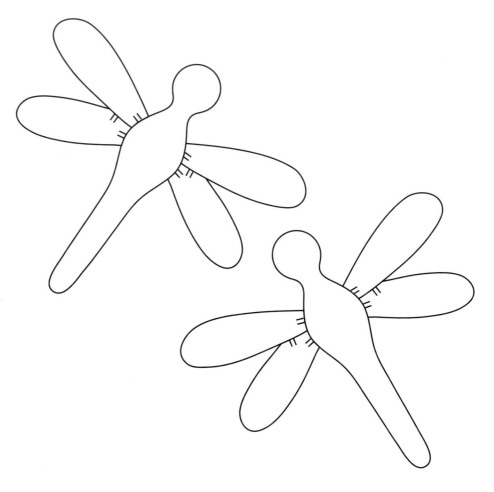

1. Choose a 6½" × 6½" square of neutral print for the background.

2. Trace 1 of each shape: body and right and left wings.

3. Fuse the body to a dark blue print.

4. Fuse all wings to the different blue print.

5. Arrange and fuse the appliqué shapes on the background. Stitch around each of the shapes with matching thread.

## Finishing

After the blocks are stitched and quilted with a simple straight crosshatching design in the background, complete the blocks as follows:

1. Press and trim each block to 5½" × 5½".

2. Bind the blocks with a 2½" (cut width) double-fold bias binding, using a ¼" seam allowance to sew the binding to the front of the block.

3. Hand stitch the binding to the back of the block.

4. Display or frame, as desired.

# MIDNIGHT IN THE GARDEN

*Midnight in the Garden*, designed by Annie Smith, Morgan Hill, California, 2008. Machine appliqué by Annie Smith and Aneda Phillips. Hand piecing and hand embroidery by Annie Smith. Quilting by Melodee Wade, Sunnyvale, California.

**Finished quilt: 36″ × 41″**

## Materials

*Refer to the list on page 26 for basic supplies.*

- Paper-backed fusible web, 37″ wide: 2 yards
- Background fabric: ⅝ yard of black solid
- Border fabric: 1¼ yards of black solid
- Sashing fabric: ⅓ yard of black-and-white print
- Dark green print for stems and some leaves: ⅝ yard
- 2 green prints, medium and light, for leaves: ¼ yard of each

- 3 purple prints in a gradation from light to dark for flowers and vase: ¼ yard of each
- 2 orange prints, light and medium, for flowers: ¼ yard of each
- 2 yellow prints, light and medium, for flowers and dots: ¼ yard of each
- 3 pink prints in a gradation from light to dark for flowers: ¼ yard of each
- 2 blue prints, light and medium, for dragonflies: ⅛ yard of each
- Embroidery floss for fuchsia tendrils and leaf stems
- 8 assorted ½″ buttons for flower center embellishment
- Batting: 44″ × 49″, or crib-size
- Backing fabric: 1⅜ yards (requires minimum 44″ fabric width)
- Binding: ⅝ yard

The patterns for the *Midnight in the Garden* center piece and border are on pattern pullout pages 1 and 2 at the back of the book. Use a 17″ × 22″ piece of tracing paper to trace the center piece and a 9″ × 22″ piece for the border. Use the traced full-size patterns or the pullout pattern to trace your appliqué shapes and draw placement lines on the center piece and the border fabrics. Instructions for stems and how to create the appliqué designs can be found in Chapter 5: Appliqué Methods (page 33).

# Instructions

## Center Piece

1. Cut a 19″ × 24″ piece of background fabric. Starch the fabric for stability.

2. From the dark green print, cut ⅞″-wide bias strips to total 49″ and prepare the stems. (Refer to Bias Stems and Vines and Tri-fold Bias Strips, page 40.)

3. Transfer the stem placement lines onto the background. Do not transfer any other designs to the background.

4. Pin and hand baste the stems to the background over the placement lines. Cut the stems to fit the placement lines after they have been basted to the background. Use the leftover stem pieces for the shorter stems.

5. Prepare all the appliqué shapes, including the vase, for the center piece. Leave the yo-yo flowers for *after* you have stitched all the other elements.

6. Arrange and fuse the appliqué shapes to the background fabric.

7. Stitch around all the elements using threads to match the fabrics. Stitch the stems with a straight stitch ¹⁄₁₆″ from the edge.

8. To make the yo-yo flowers, refer to page 104.

9. Hand stitch the yo-yo flowers in place on the background fabric, using a blind hem stitch.

10. Embroider the stems and flower tendrils indicated by dashed lines on the pattern, using 2 strands of embroidery floss and a stem stitch.

11. After completing all the stitching, press and trim the center piece to 17½″ × 22½″. Make sure the design is centered before trimming. You will have approximately 1″–2″ of fabric around all the appliqué elements.

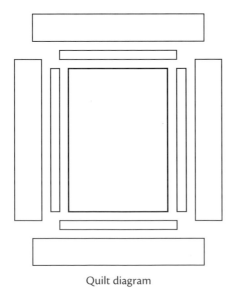

Quilt diagram

## Sashing

1. From the sashing fabric, cut 2 strips 2½″ × 17½″ and 2 strips 2½″ × 26½″.

2. Pin and sew the 17½″ sashing strips to the top and bottom of the center piece. Press the seams toward the sashing.

3. Pin and sew the 26½″ strips to each side of the center piece. Press the seams toward the sashing.

## Side Borders

1. Cut 2 strips of border fabric 9½″ × 28″.

2. From the dark green print, cut ⅞″-wide bias strips to total 120″ and prepare the stems. (Refer to Bias Stems and Vines and Tri-fold Bias Strips, page 40.) This amount is sufficient for all 4 borders.

3. Pin the large 3-layer flower in the center of the border. Mark the stem lines on the border piece. Use the center flower as a placement guide; it will be fused in place *last*.

4. Hand baste the stems over the marked lines, beginning at the flower center.

5. Allow the stem piece that extends past the end of the border to dangle, as it will be connected to the top or bottom border piece once you sew the borders onto the center piece. The small corner 3-layer flowers that are attached to those stems will be fused and stitched to the borders *last*.

**Note** When adding appliqué elements to the border pieces, keep in mind that the borders will be trimmed to the following sizes after all the stitching is complete:

Side borders: 8″ × 26½″

Top and bottom borders: 8″ × 36½″

Remember to leave at least ½″ for the seam allowance around the outside edge of the appliqué elements.

6. Once the stems are basted in place, you can add the rest of the appliqué elements for the border pieces.

7. Add and fuse dandelion leaves on either side of the large center flower.

8. Add and fuse 10 heart-shaped leaves, 10 dots, and 2 dragonflies.

9. Stack, fuse, and stitch the center circles of the center 3-layer flower before fusing the flower over the stems and tucked edges of the dandelion leaves.

10. Stitch around each of the appliqué elements.

11. Press and trim the completed side border strips to 8″ × 26½″, centering the appliqué before trimming.

## Top and Bottom Borders

1. Cut 2 strips of border fabric 9½″ × 38″.

2. Follow Steps 3, 4, and 6–10 in Side Borders (page 80 and above). Note that the top and bottom borders have 12 heart-shaped leaves each.

3. Layer the posy and calyx in place at the end of each stem and fuse in place.

4. Add the teardrops that go on top of the posy and fuse.

5. Add the small dots and fuse.

6. Stitch around each of the appliqué elements.

7. Press the completed top and bottom border pieces and trim to 8″ × 36½″, centering the appliqué before trimming.

## Sewing on the Borders

1. Sew the borders to the sides of the center piece first and press the seams toward the borders.

2. Attach the top and bottom borders next and press the seams toward the borders.

3. Hand baste the dangling stems from the side borders to the top and bottom borders.

4. Stack, fuse, and stitch the centers of the small corner flowers. Fuse them in place on the borders, covering the ends of the stems, and stitch around the outer edges of the flowers.

5. Stitch all the stem pieces using a matching thread and a straight stitch 1/16″ from the edge.

6. Don't forget to add the embroidered stems (indicated by dashed lines) to the heart-shaped leaves on the border pieces.

Your quilt is now ready for quilting!

## Binding

Cut 2¾″-wide bias strips to make binding for your quilt. You need approximately 154″ of binding. Add at least an extra 24″ of binding for diagonal joins of the binding ends for a total of 178″ of bias strips.

# GREENHOUSE

*Greenhouse*, Annie Smith, Morgan Hill, California, 2009. Quilting by Marty Vint of Dogwood Quilting, Baltimore, Maryland.

**Finished quilt:** 62″ × 62″

## Materials

*Refer to the list on page 26 for basic supplies. I used batik fabrics for the background, sashing, and borders, and Cherrywood hand-dyes (see Resources, page 156) for all the appliqué. You can reproduce the look of this quilt by using solid fabrics, or use printed fabrics for a completely different look. Cherrywood hand-dyes come in fat-quarter packs, so the materials list for the appliqué assumes fat-quarter measurements. Prewash hand-dyes with Synthrapol prior to using them so the color will not run when the quilt is washed.*

- Paper-backed fusible web, 37″ wide: 3 yards
- Background fabric: 2½ yards of light green
- Border and center piece fabric: 3⅛ yards of green
- Sashing: 1⅓ yards of lavender
- Dark green for stems: 1 yard
- 3 greens for leaves: 1 fat quarter of each
- 3 blues in a gradation from light to dark: 1 fat quarter of each
- 3 purples in a gradation from light to dark: 1 fat quarter of each
- 2 oranges, light and medium: 1 fat quarter of each
- 2 yellows, light and medium: 1 fat quarter of each
- 3 rosy pinks in a gradation from light to dark: 1 fat quarter of each
- 3 rusts in a gradation from light to dark: 1 fat quarter of each
- 3 fabrics in a gradation from medium gray to charcoal gray to black: 1 fat quarter of each
- Red: 1 fat quarter
- Batting: 2 yards of 108″-wide batting of your choice (I used Mathilda's wool for this quilt.)
- Backing fabric: 4½ yards
- Binding: Use the leftover background fabric.

The *Greenhouse* block patterns are found on pages 84–100. (The dashed lines on the patterns indicate possible embellishments.) The *Greenhouse* center piece and border patterns are on pattern pullout pages 1 and 2 at the back of the book. Use 10″ × 10″ squares of tracing paper to trace each of the blocks, a 20″ × 20″ square for the center block, and a 12″ × 36″ piece for the border. Use the full-size traced patterns or the pullout pattern to trace your appliqué shapes. Draw placement lines on the center piece and borders. Instructions for the stems and how to create the appliqué designs are in Chapter 5: Appliqué Methods (page 33).

VIOLETS: half of asymmetrical
design. Use fusible rather than bias
to create stems in this design.

Pattern is shown reversed for
machine appliqué.

VIOLETS: half of asymmetrical design. Use fusible rather than bias to create stems in this design.

Pattern is shown reversed for machine appliqué.

For correct placement of this shape, rotate pattern 180° before tracing second half.

MERRY-GO-ROUND: half of symmetrical design

LANTANA: half of
symmetrical design

STRING OF HEARTS: half of
asymmetrical design

Pattern is shown reversed for
machine appliqué.

STRING OF HEARTS: half of
asymmetrical design

Pattern is shown reversed for
machine appliqué.

BUGS AND BUTTERFLIES: half of
asymmetrical design

Pattern is shown reversed for
machine appliqué.

BUGS AND BUTTERFLIES: half of asymmetrical design

Pattern is shown reversed for machine appliqué.

TULIPS: half of asymmetrical design

Pattern is shown reversed for machine appliqué.

TULIPS: half of asymmetrical design

Pattern is shown reversed for machine appliqué.

NOSEGAY: half of symmetrical design

For correct stem placement, rotate pattern 180° before tracing second half.

CARNATIONS: half of symmetrical design

ORANGE BLOSSOM HONEY:
half of asymmetrical design

Pattern is shown reversed for
machine appliqué.

ORANGE BLOSSOM HONEY:
half of asymmetrical design

Pattern is shown reversed for
machine appliqué.

RING OF ROSEBUDS: half of
symmetrical design

STAR FLOWER: half of
symmetrical design

Use fusible rather than bias to
create stems in this design.

POSIES: half of symmetrical design

## Cutting and Fusing Instructions

### Blocks

1. Cut 12 squares 12″ × 12″ of background fabric. Starch the fabric squares for stability.

2. Transfer the stem placement lines onto the background for the String of Hearts, Carnations, Tulips, and Posies blocks. It's not necessary to transfer stem lines for any of the other designs.

3. Cut ⅞″-wide bias strips to total approximately 80″ and prepare the stems for all the blocks except Violets and Star Flower; these use fused stems. (Refer to Stem and Vines: Fused or Bias?, pages 40–42.)

4. Hand baste the bias stems to the blocks over the placement lines. Fuse the stems for Violets and Star Flower.

5. Prepare all the appliqué shapes for each block.

6. Fuse the elements that are single, such as leaves or dots. Layer the tucked elements and fuse in place.

7. Fuse any stacked elements, such as flowers, and stitch their centers with matching threads prior to fusing them to the background.

8. Stitch around all the elements using threads that match the fabrics. Stitch the bias stems with a straight stitch ¹⁄₁₆″ from the edge; use the blanket stitch for the fused stems in Violets and Star Flower.

After completing all the stitching, remove the basting stitches. Press and trim each block to 10½″ × 10½″. Be sure the appliqué is centered before trimming.

### Center Piece

1. Cut 1 square 22″ × 22″ of border fabric. Starch the fabric for stability.

2. Cut ⅞″-wide bias strips to total 120″ and prepare the stems. (Refer to Bias Stems and Vines and Tri-fold Bias Strips, page 40.)

3. Transfer the stem placement lines onto the background. Do not transfer any other designs to the background.

4. Hand baste the stems to the background over the placement lines. Cut the stems to fit the placement lines after they have been basted to the background. Use the leftover stem pieces for the shorter stems.

5. Prepare all the appliqué shapes.

6. Fuse the elements that are single, such as leaves or dots. Layer the tucked elements and fuse in place.

7. Fuse any stacked elements, such as flowers, and stitch their centers with matching threads prior to fusing them to the background.

8. Stitch around all the elements using threads that match the fabrics. Stitch the stems with a straight stitch ¹⁄₁₆″ from the edge.

After completing all the stitching, remove the basting stitches. Press and trim the center piece to 20½″ × 20½″. Be sure the appliqué is centered before trimming.

## Assembly

Following the layout grid below, lay out the blocks on a design wall to decide where each block needs to be.

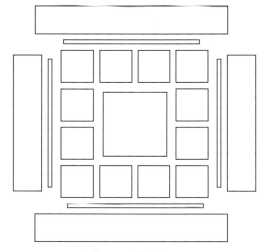

Quilt assembly diagram

Now look at color balance and block design balance to make sure the quilt is not heavy in any area.

*Before sewing the finished units together,* you have the opportunity to add some free-motion machine or hand embroidery detail to the flowers and leaves. Refer to Chapter 11: Options for Appliqué Elements and Embellishments (page 104).

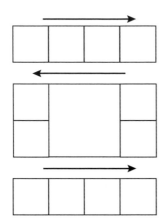

Center section layout: arrows indicate pressing direction.

1. Sew together the 2 sets of side blocks. Sew 1 set to each side of the center piece. Press.

2. Sew the top 4 blocks together. Press.

3. Sew the top 4-block set to the top of the center section. Press.

4. Sew the bottom 4 blocks together. Press.

5. Sew the bottom 4-block set to the bottom of the center section. Press.

## Sashing

1. Cut 2 strips 1½″ × 40½″ of sashing fabric.

2. Sew the sashing strips to each side of the center section. Press the seams toward the sashing.

3. Cut 2 strips 1½″ × 42½″ of sashing fabric.

4. Sew the sashing strips to the top and bottom of the center section. Press the seams toward the sashing.

## Borders

When adding appliqué elements to the border pieces, keep in mind that the borders will be trimmed after all the stitching is completed. Leave enough room around the appliqué elements for a ¼″ seam allowance on all sides.

1. Cut 2 strips 12″ × 44″ of border fabric for the sides.

2. Cut 2 strips 12″ × 64″ of border fabric for the top and bottom.

3. From the dark green print, cut ⅞″-wide bias strips to total approximately 370″. Prepare the stems from the bias strips. (Refer to Bias Stems and Vines and Tri-fold Bias Strips, page 40.)

4. Use the pattern to mark all the stem placement lines for the side borders, centering the pattern on the border fabric.

5. Pin and hand baste the stems over the marked lines, beginning near the heart center. Trim after basting the stems in place so the length will be correct.

6. Prepare the appliqué elements. Fuse the elements in place. The elements for the side borders are single units or tucked flowers, so there will be no stacked-element stitching on these borders.

7. Stitch around all the appliqué pieces with matching thread. Stitch all the stem pieces with a straight stitch 1⁄16″ from the edge.

8. Free-motion stitch or embroider the stems and dots that embellish the tops of the flowers, as indicated by dashed lines on the patterns.

9. Remove all the basting threads.

10. Press the side border pieces and trim to 10½″ × 42½″. Be sure the appliqué is centered before trimming.

11. Sew a side border to each side of the center section, placing the bottom of the heart toward the center section. Press the seam allowances toward the border.

12. Press the top and bottom border pieces and trim to 10½″ × 62½″.

13. Sew the remaining borders to the top and bottom of the center section. Press the seam allowances toward the border.

Your quilt is now ready for quilting!!

## Binding

Cut 2¾″-wide bias strips to make binding for the quilt. You need approximately 248″ of binding. Add at least an extra 24″ of binding for diagonal joins of the binding ends for a total of 272″ of bias strips.

# CHAPTER 10

# How to Use Appliqué Templates

## Using the Appliqué Elements with Other Resources

There are many books that have pictures of appliqué quilts in them but that have no patterns for the appliqué shapes and elements. Use the templates found in this guidebook to create your own patterns.

Another book that will be a help to you in the design process is Barbara Brackman's *Encyclopedia of Appliqué,* which has traditional and modern designs for appliqué blocks. The templates in my guidebook will work well with the patterns in the *Encyclopedia.*

## Other Types of Appliqué

The appliqué shapes and motifs offered in this book, while presented under the title of fine appliqué, can also be used and adapted for any other type of appliqué. This is a resource book for you. You can use any of the designs in this book to embellish a sweatshirt, a jacket, or any other article of clothing; to decorate a board book; or in any other instance when you want to appliqué.

Craft appliqué is meant to be used for a limited amount of time (such as while the piece of clothing fits or the tea towel is useful). Any fabric appliqué shapes that can be permanently affixed to a flat background can also be used for a three-dimensional shape, such as wearable art. Just keep the fusible web underneath the entire appliqué; don't cut it away.

## Mix and Match

All the appliqué designs in this book are meant to allow you to play and come up with your own designs. There are pages of multisize flowers, leaves, stars, and other elements that will allow you to create your own appliqué elements. Various sizes of circles can be found within the design elements to use wherever you wish.

Try putting a flower inside a large circle, or surround a series of diminishing circles with a scalloped flower. Try a flower with a circle and star center. You can swap calyxes, stamens, and other design details with flower shapes to create something new.

I hope you'll be interested in finding out what you can create using this guidebook. I would love to see what you create. Please send a picture of your quilt to me at annie@simplearts.com.

# CHAPTER 11

## Options for Appliqué Elements and Embellishments

# Adding Appliqué to a Pieced Quilt

If you have a pieced quilt that you haven't quilted yet because you just didn't like the way it turned out, why not add appliqué to it?

### In the Quilt

Make some pieced blocks and intermingle them with some appliquéd blocks. Try turning your blocks on-point for a different view.

### On the Quilt

Appliqué flowers or a meandering vine on the main part of the quilt can add a beautiful accent.

### On the Border

Add appliqué to a pieced border or to a quiet print border. The key to having your appliqué show is using appliqué fabrics that are darker in value than the pieced or printed portion of the border.

### As a Border

Create a unique border for a pieced quilt by making your borders completely with appliqué on a solid piece of background fabric. You can use one of the borders from the pattern pullout pages at the back of the book or design your own.

### To Repair a Quilt

Appliqué on top of piecework is beautiful and can cover up a mistake or a stain, and no one will be the wiser. It's also a great way to repair a tear in a quilt, especially if you have some leftover fabrics. If the quilt has aged, tea-dye the appliqué fabric to match the quilt.

# Adding Embroidery

Adding machine or hand embroidery to appliqué is a nice to way to add texture and depth to your quilt. Add a vein to a leaf, swirls to flower petals, flight motion marks to a bird or dragonfly, dots on a ladybug, or anything you can dream up!

For ideas on hand embroidery, I like Judith Baker Montano's *Embroidery & Crazy Quilt Stitch Tool* (see page 160).

Many of my patterns include suggestions for embroidery embellishment. They are indicated on the patterns by dashed lines. Refer to the project photos for additional ideas.

## Free-Motion Embroidery

You will need an open-toe darning foot that has a spring in it. The open toe will allow you to have a clear view of where and how you are stitching.

You will also need to drop the feed dogs on your sewing machine so the fabric can glide smoothly under the foot.

I practice doodling on a scrap piece of fabric prior to stitching on my actual appliqué pieces. Hold the fabric taut and flat, but don't stretch it. When you feel comfortable with the smooth motion of your practice stitching, you're ready to add your own embellishment to your appliqué. After adding free-motion embroidery work to the piece, press the area to flatten any distortion before proceeding.

# Adding Yo-yos

Yo-yos are one of my favorite embellishments to add to any quilt. I use the Clover yo-yo maker tool, which comes in a variety of sizes and makes a perfect yo-yo every time.

# CHAPTER 12

# Catalog of Appliqué Design Elements

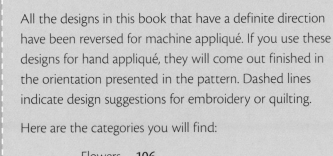

All the designs in this book that have a definite direction have been reversed for machine appliqué. If you use these designs for hand appliqué, they will come out finished in the orientation presented in the pattern. Dashed lines indicate design suggestions for embroidery or quilting.

Here are the categories you will find:

# Flowers
## Stacked Flowers

Simple six-curve flower

Four-layer eight-curve flower

Simple five-curve flower

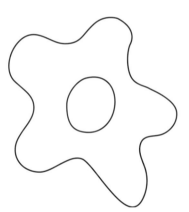

Five-point flower

Small six-curve flower

Three-layer eight-curve flower

Cornflower

Three-layer twelve-curve flower

Three-layer five-point flower

Four-layer eight-scallop flower

Layered eight-curve and scallop flower

Hibiscus

Eight-curve and ring flower

Dahlia

Marigold

Plumeria

Snowdrop

Peek-a-boo

Russian rose

Drum flower

Posy in a posy

# Tucked Flowers

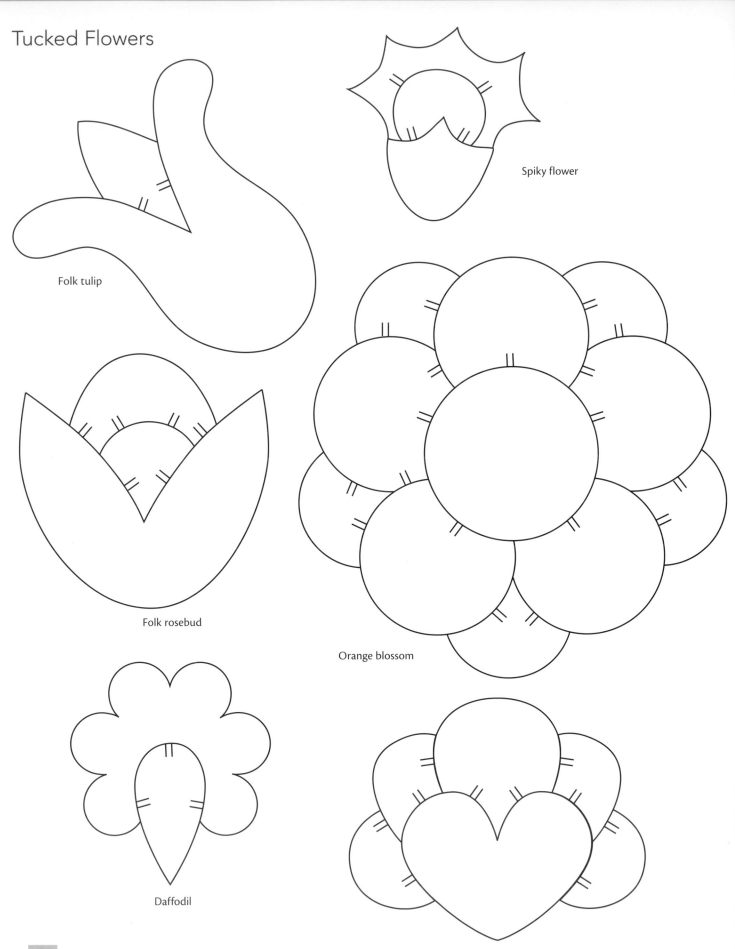

Spiky flower

Folk tulip

Folk rosebud

Orange blossom

Daffodil

Blossoming heart

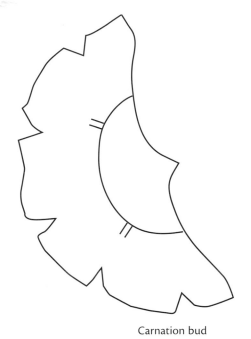

Carnation bud

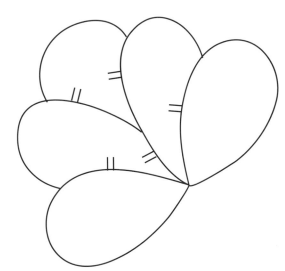

Five-petal flower

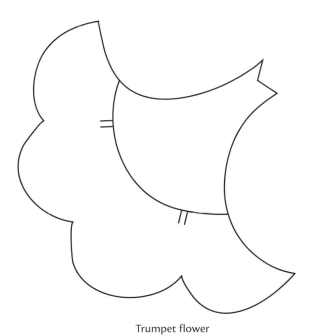

Trumpet flower

Heart flower

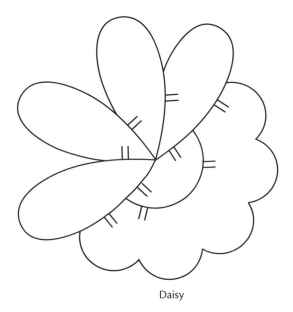

Daisy

Iris

Pansy

Gerbera daisy

Fuchsia

Lady's slipper

Orchid

Stephanotis

Anthurium

Bluebell

Gladiolus

# Combination Flowers

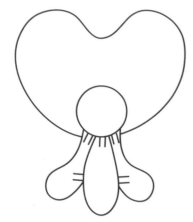

Bleeding heart

Crocus

Ringed posy

Lily of the valley

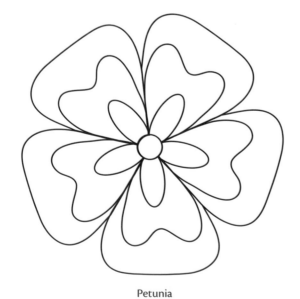

Petunia

Six-curve flower with petals

Scottish rose

Pop flower on a stem

Heart flower on a stem

Belladonna

Violet

Jasmine

Dianthus

Hydrangea

Jonquil

Buttercup

Sunflower

Flower power

Deco lily

Columbine

Deco tulip

Folk rose

Carnation

Deco tulip

Whimsical tulip

Merry-go-round

Whimsical daisy

# Flower Buds

Three rosebuds

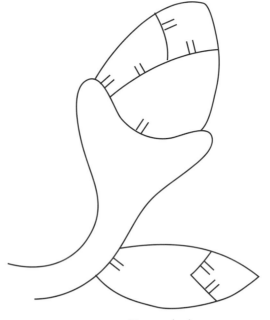

Two rosebuds

Single bud

Paradise bud

Bud with leaves

Round bud

Detached buds

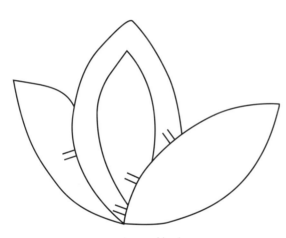

Layered bud

Crocus bud

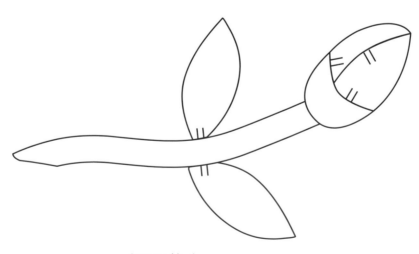

Stemmed bud

# Leaves

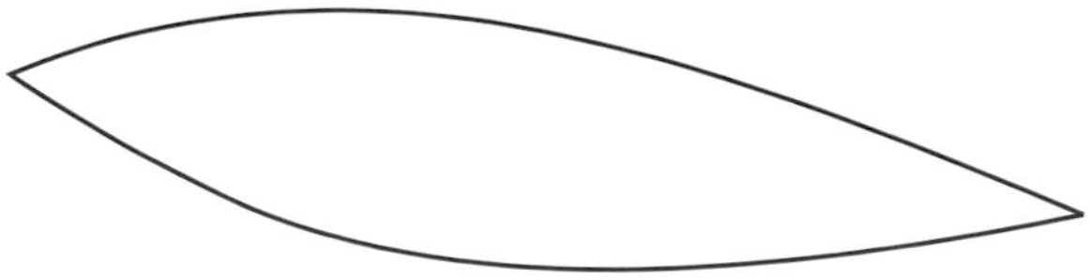

Tulip leaf

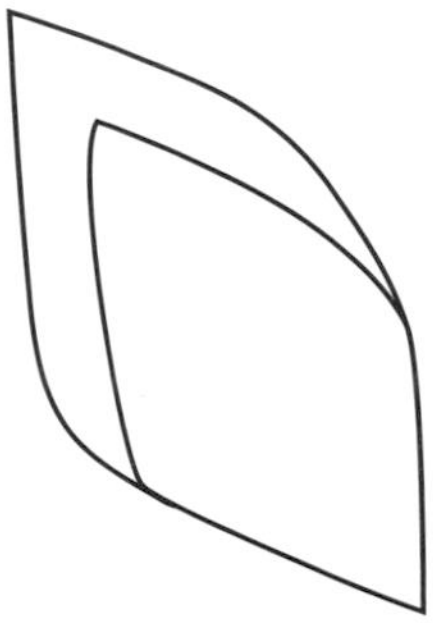

Bare leaf

Piped leaf

Slender leaf

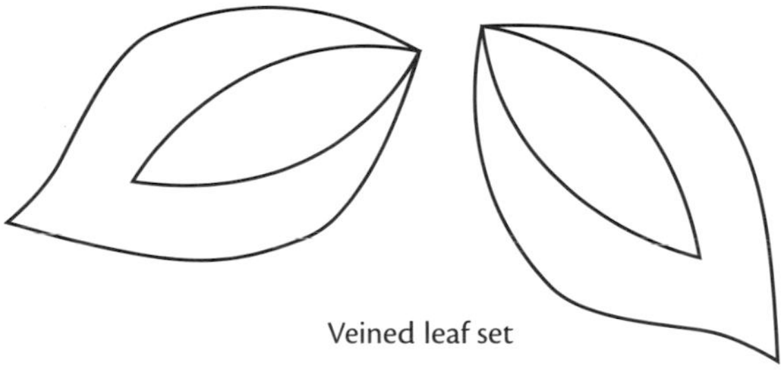

Veined leaf set

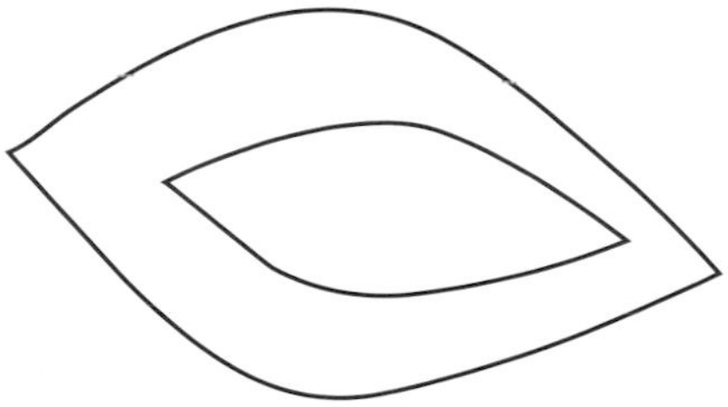

Simple leaf

Detached veined leaf

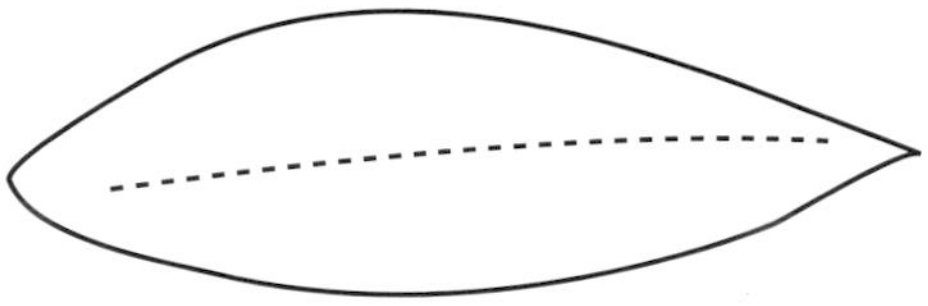

Curled leaf

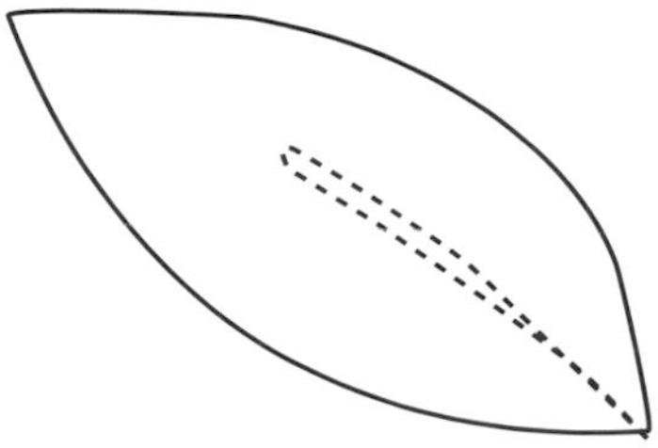

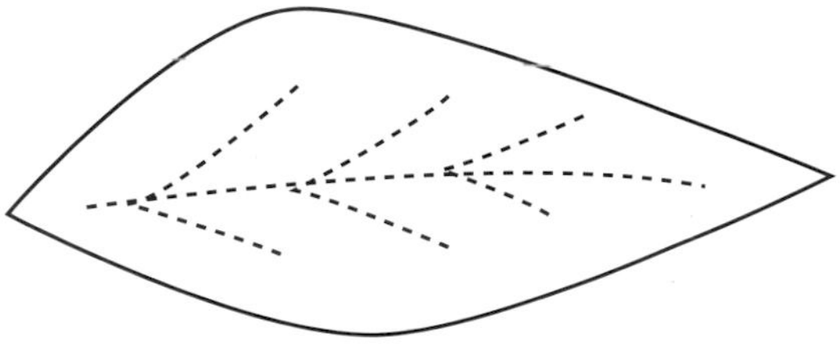

Almond-shaped leaf

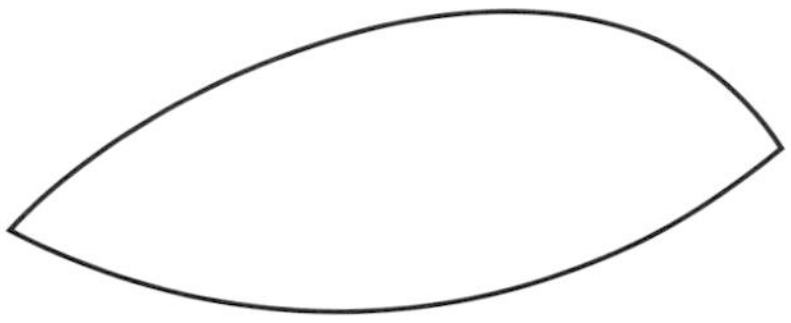

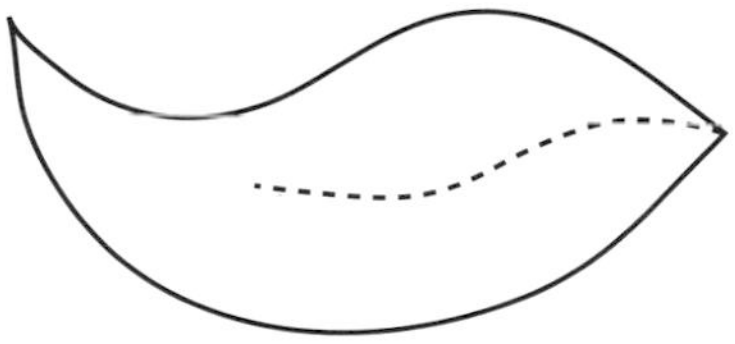

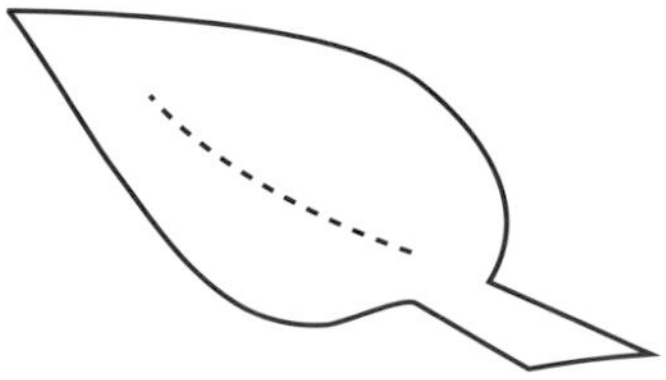

Leaf with stem

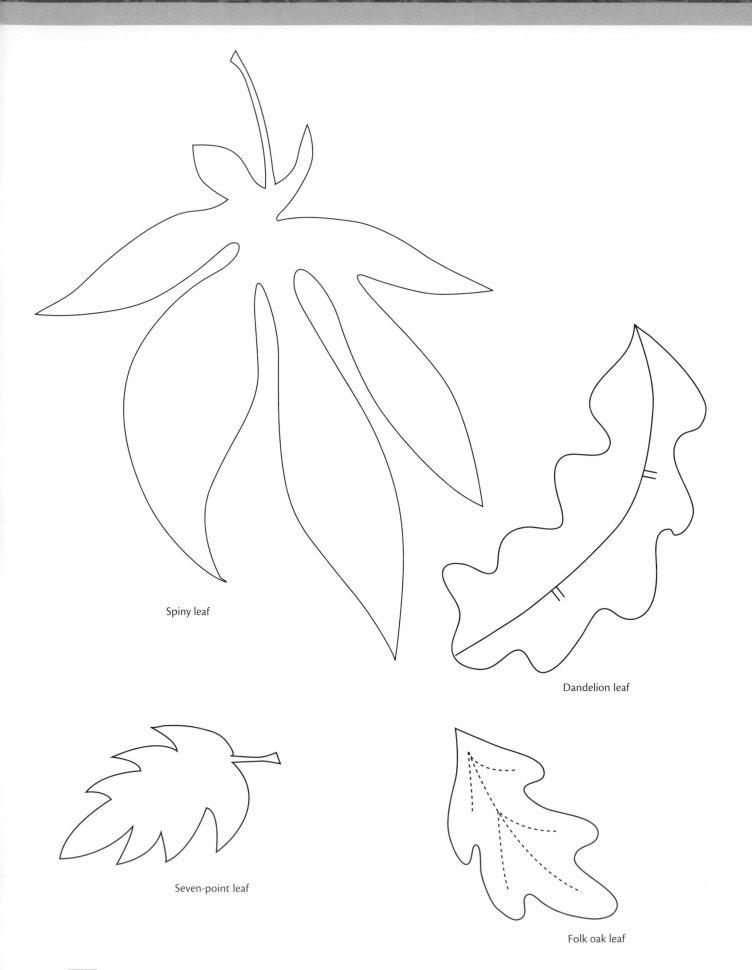

Spiny leaf

Dandelion leaf

Seven-point leaf

Folk oak leaf

Stacked heart leaf

Scattered leaves

Leaf trio

Philodendron leaves

Veined whimsical leaf

Veined oak leaf

Acanthus

Traditional maple leaf

Tucked almond leaf

Leaf cluster

Teardrop leaf set

Triad leaf

Heart-shaped leaf

New leaf

Nouveau leaf trio

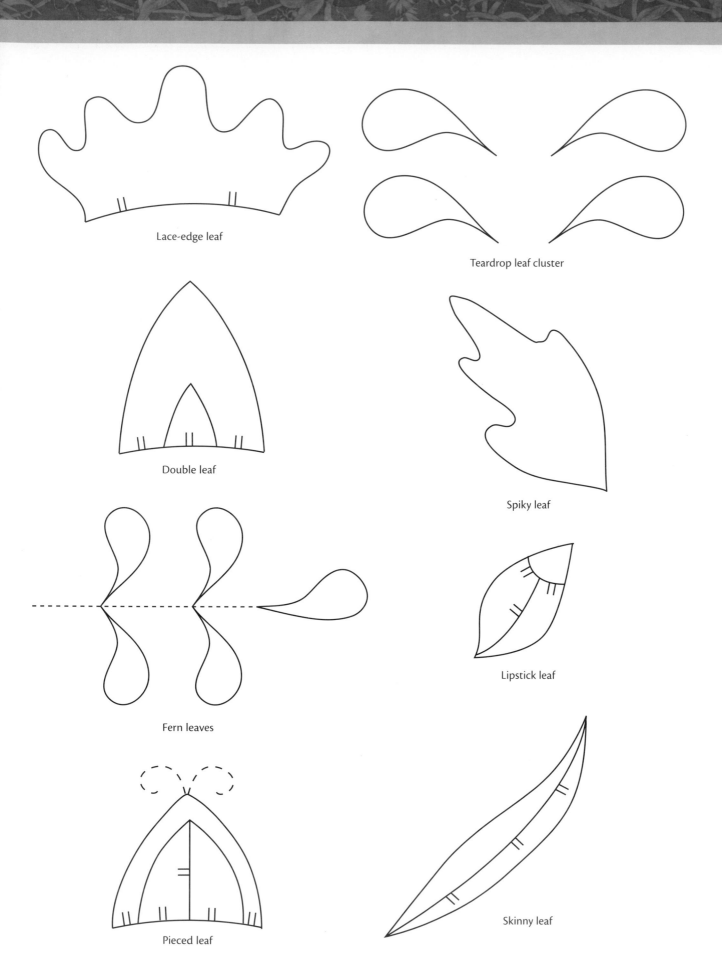

Lace-edge leaf

Teardrop leaf cluster

Double leaf

Spiky leaf

Fern leaves

Lipstick leaf

Pieced leaf

Skinny leaf

Leaf vine

# Containers

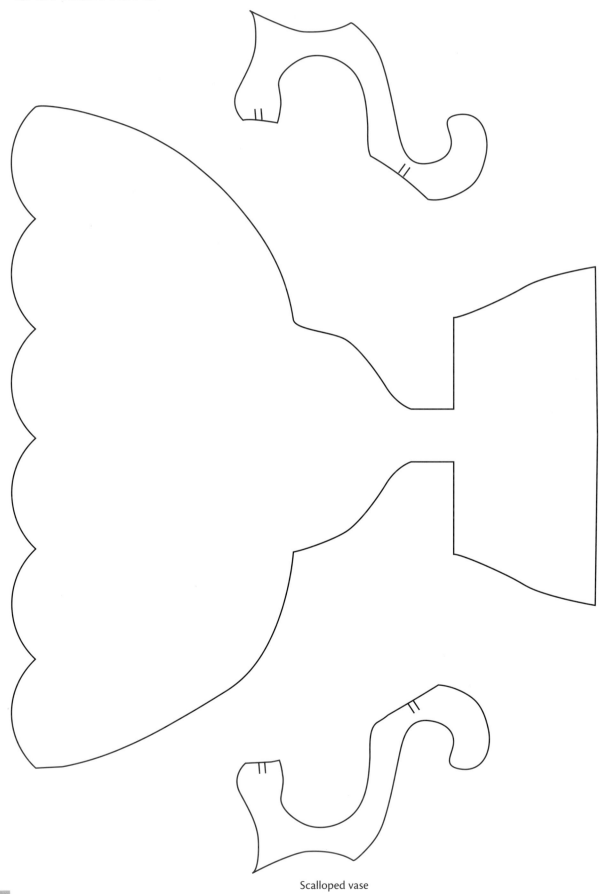

Scalloped vase

Nouveau vase

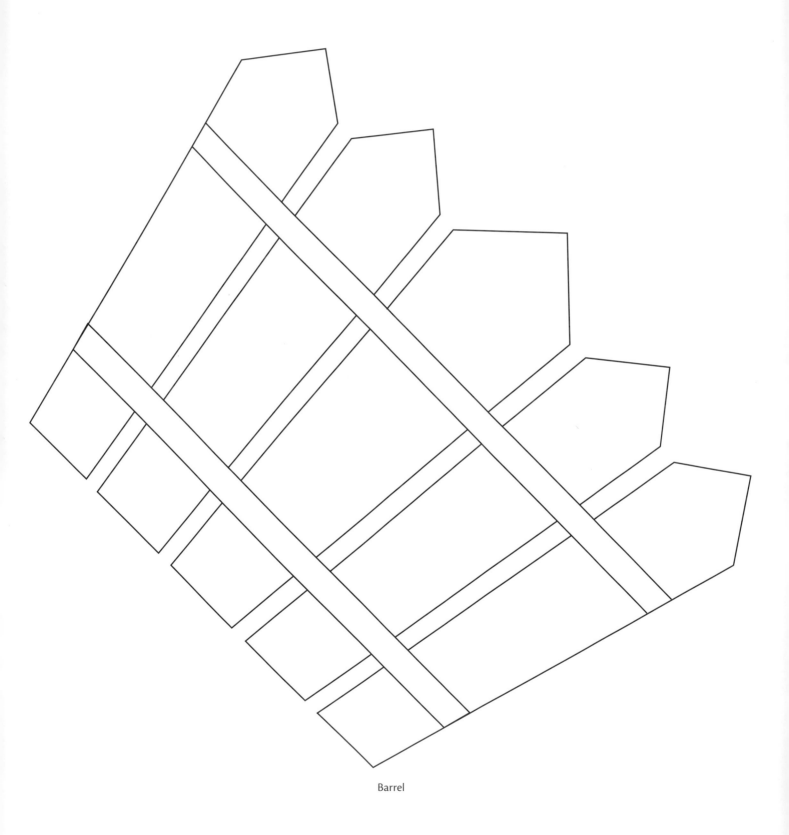

Barrel

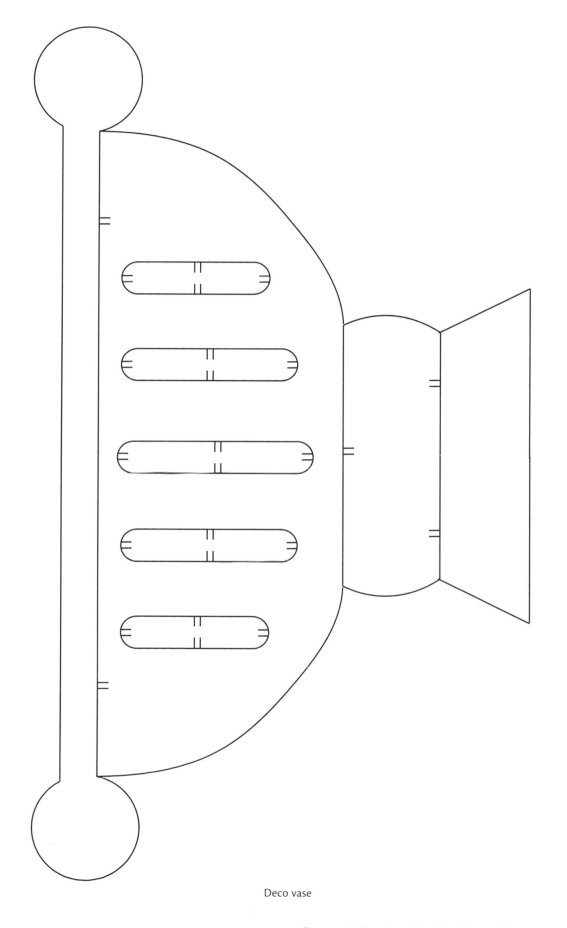

Deco vase

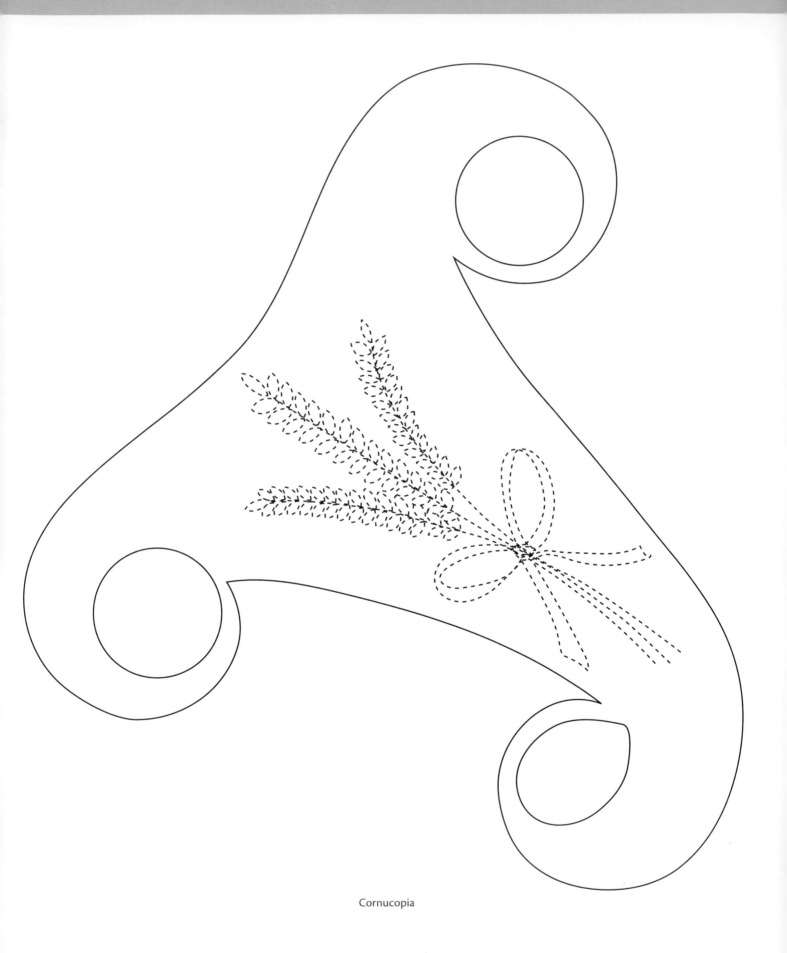

Cornucopia

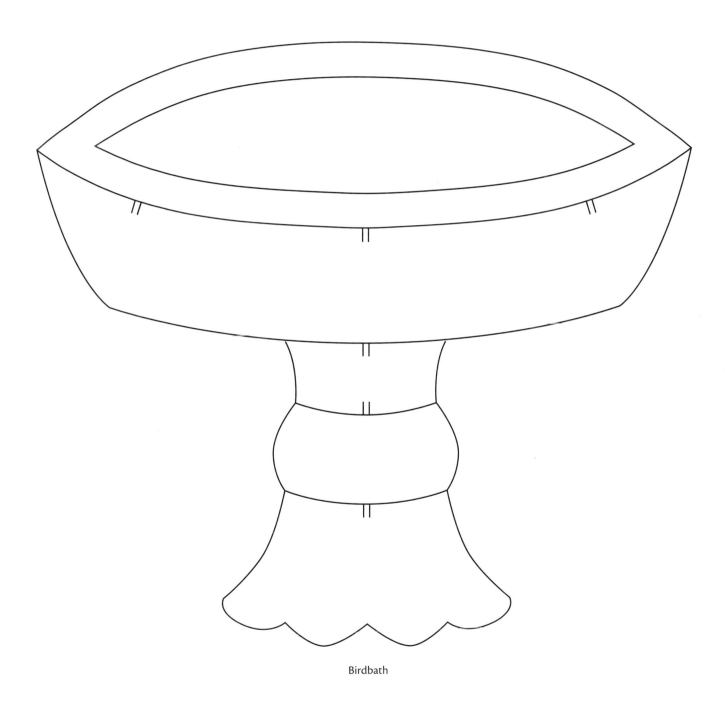

Birdbath

Basket

# Animals, Insects, and Fowl Friends

Small bumblebee

Folk bee

Simple bird

Large bumblebee

Folk ladybug

Butterfly

Whimsical ladybug

Moth

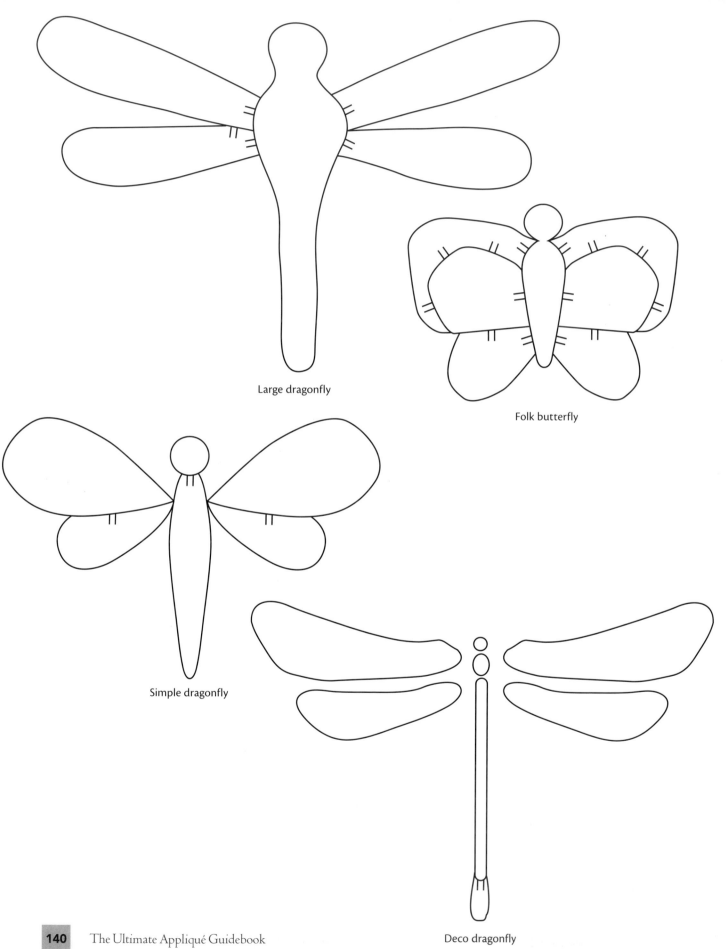

Large dragonfly

Folk butterfly

Simple dragonfly

Deco dragonfly

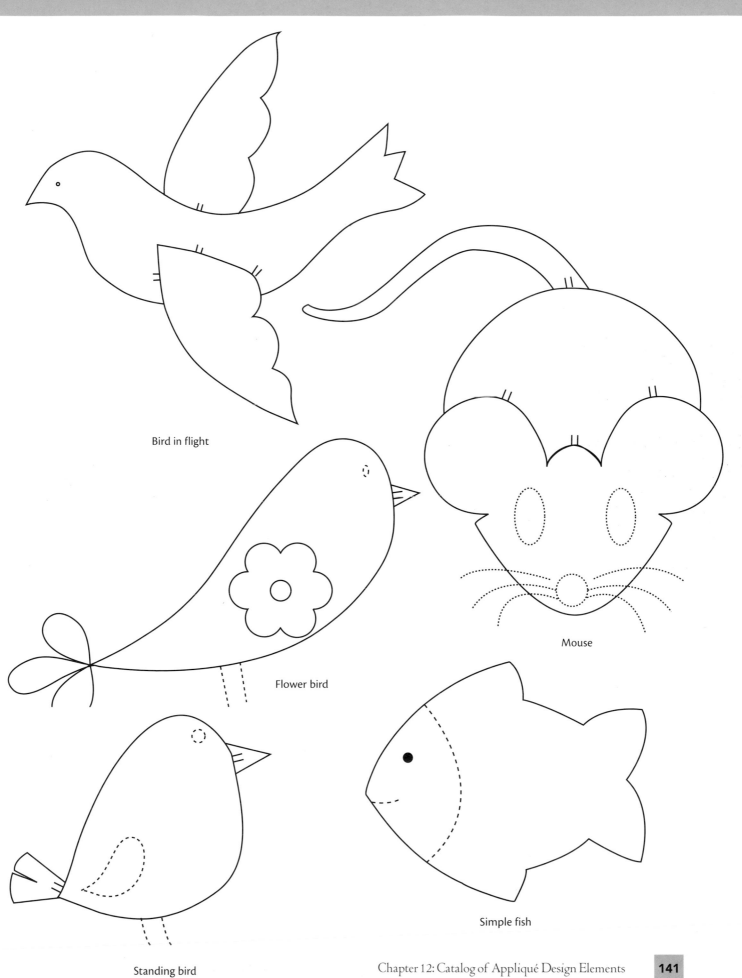

Bird in flight

Flower bird

Mouse

Standing bird

Simple fish

Feline

Bowser

Bone

# Fruit

Three cherries

Heart-shaped cherries

Whimsical pomegranate

Cherry branch

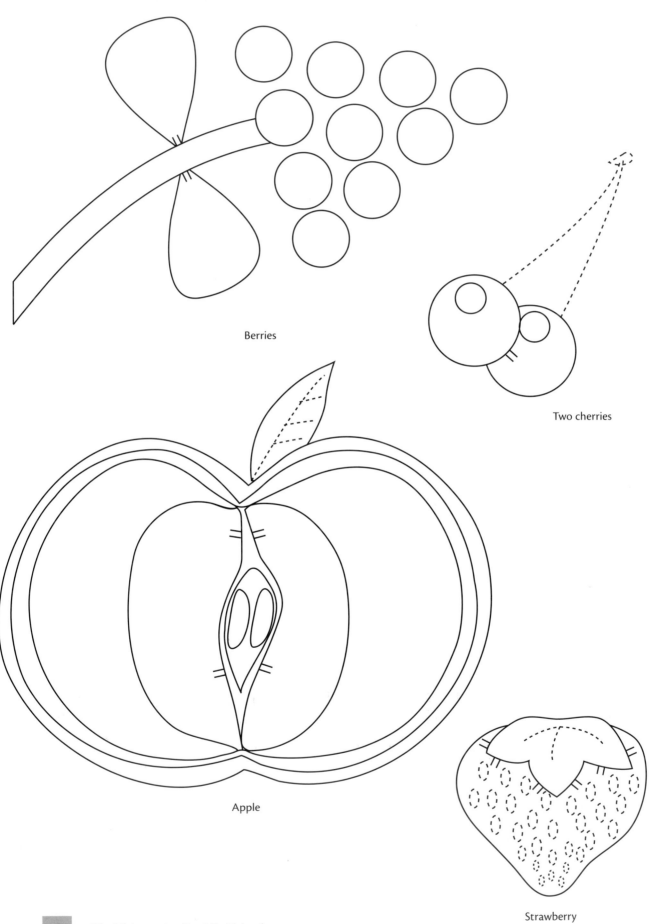

Berries

Two cherries

Apple

Strawberry

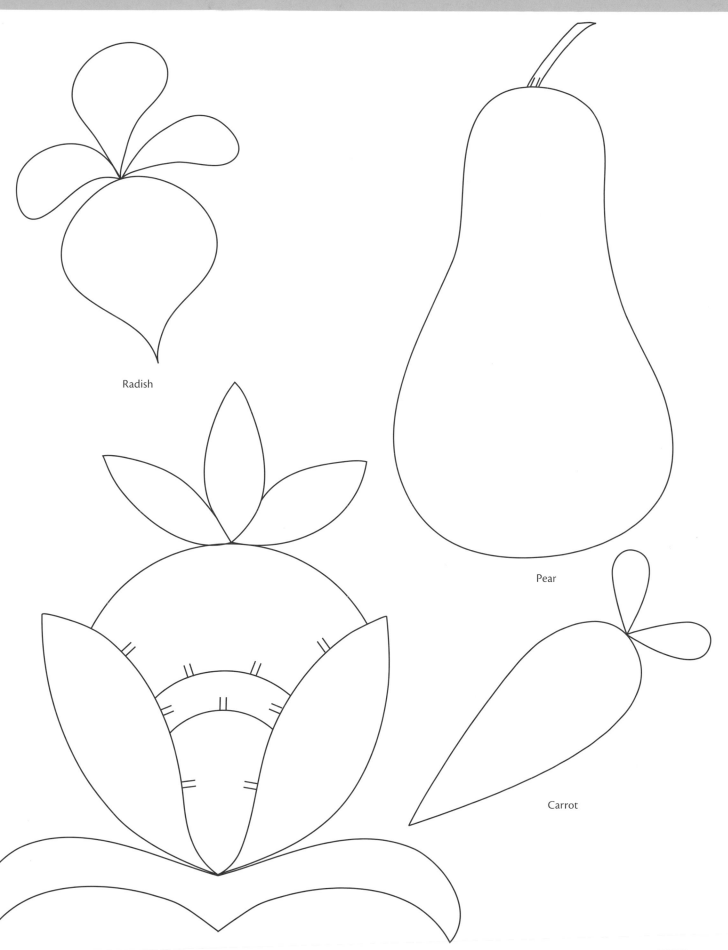

Radish

Pear

Carrot

Folk pomegranate with leaf

Watermelon

Whimsical apple

Folk pomegranate with pod

# Stars and Other Patriotic Elements

Six-point star

Small seven-point star

Twelve-point star

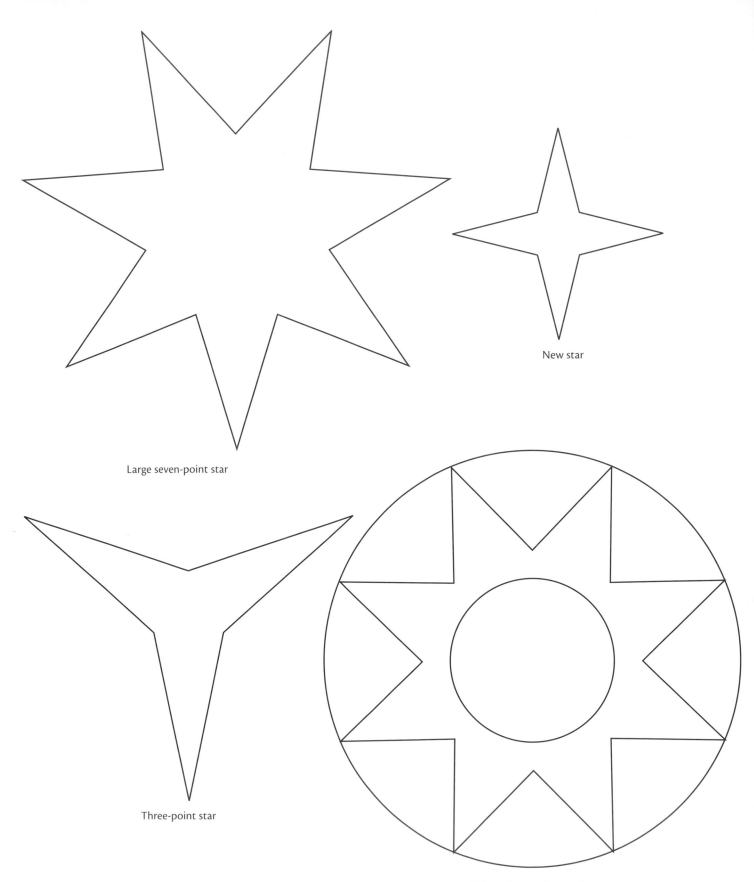

Large seven-point star

New star

Three-point star

Eight-point star in a circle

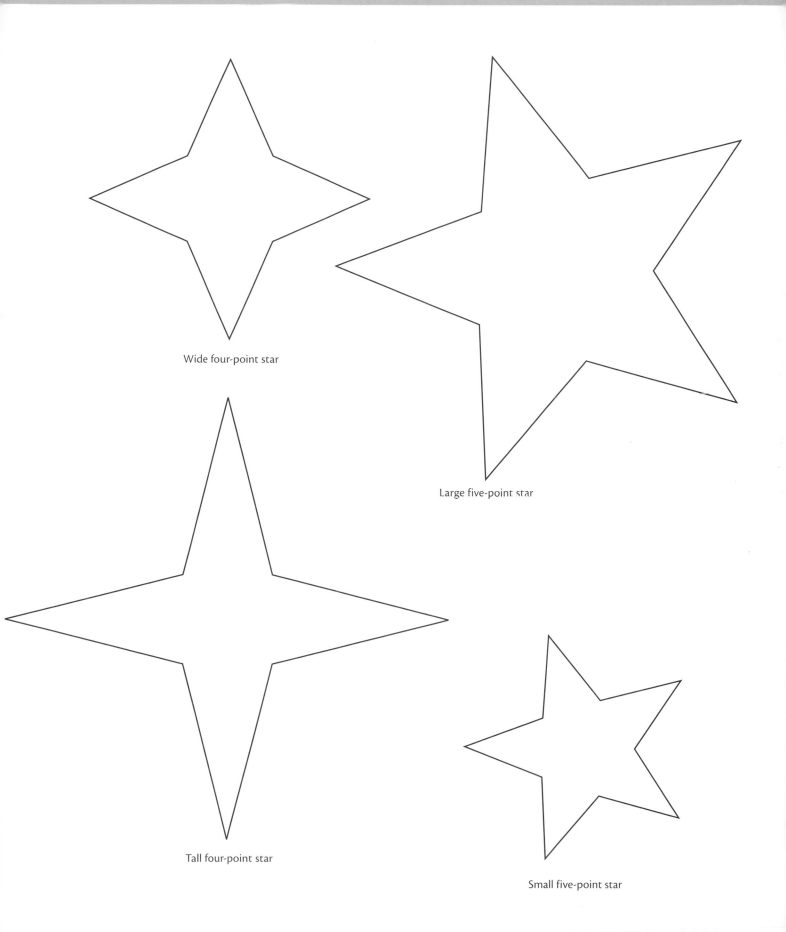

Wide four-point star

Large five-point star

Tall four-point star

Small five-point star

# Royal Design Elements

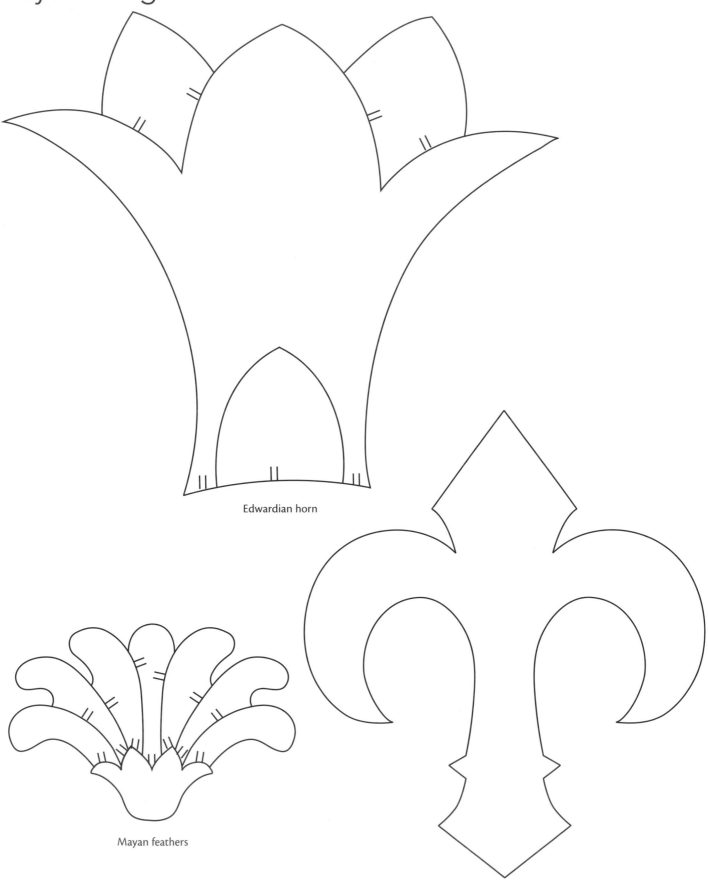

Edwardian horn

Mayan feathers

Fleur-de-lis

Cockscomb

Artichoke

# Medallions

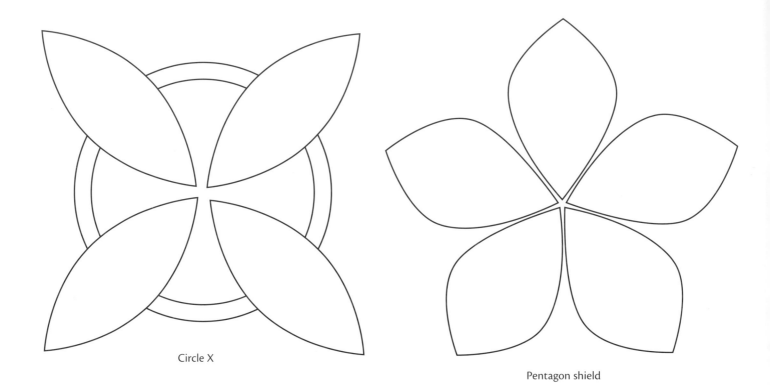

Circle X

Pentagon shield

Circle cross

Octet

Mill wheel

Heart shield

# Definitions

 **Elements**

The appliqué shapes and patterns found in this book. Each element can be combined with others to create a whole design; for example, a stem, a flower, and two leaves create a whole flower. Many elements have more than one piece that creates the design. Some elements are singular, such as a leaf, while others have pieces that stack on top of a larger foundation shape, or pieces that tuck underneath the main shape.

 **Stacked**

Flowers or elements with smaller pieces on top of the base piece.

 **Tucked**

Pieces that attach by being tucked underneath flowers or elements. This is indicated by a double dash on the pattern.

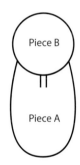

Tuck top edge of piece A under bottom edge of piece B.

 **Layer**

An element placed on top of another, such as a flower placed on top of the end of a stem to cover the raw edge.

 **Release paper**

The paper side of fusible web. After one side of the web is fused to a piece of appliqué fabric, the paper is removed to expose the other side of the web in order to fuse the appliqué element to another element or the background fabric.

 **Zig**

The zig is the cycle of the stitch that goes from the background *into* the appliqué.

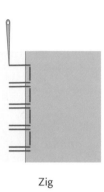

Zig

 **Zag**

The zag is the cycle of the stitch that goes *out* of the appliqué into the background.

Zag

 **Surgeon's knot**

A knot made by taking two wraps in the first stage of the knot and then one wrap for the second stage.

 **Pivoting**

Turning with the needle in the down position when you stitch the curve of an appliqué shape. Lift the presser foot and slightly turn (pivot) the piece so the next stitch will be made right along the edge of the appliqué—or so the zig stitch will be perpendicular to the edge.

 **Tuck marks**

A double dash mark on the edge of a pattern piece to indicate an edge that should be tucked under another piece.

# Bibliography

Allen, Gloria Seaman, and Nancy Gibson Tuckhorn. *A Maryland Album*. Nashville, Tennessee: Thomas Nelson Publisher, 1995.

Aug, Bobbie, Sharon Newman, and Gerald Roy. *Vintage Quilts: Identifying, Collecting, Dating, Preserving and Valuing*. Paducah, Kentucky: Collector Books, 2002.

Baker Montano, Judith. Embroidery & Crazy Quilt Stitch Tool. Lafayette, California: C&T Publishing, 2008.

Brackman, Barbara. *Encyclopedia of Appliqué*. Lafayette, California: C&T Publishing, 2009.

---. *Prairie Flower: A Year on the Plains*. Kansas City, Missouri: Kansas City Star, 2001.

Crews, Patricia Cox, ed. *A Flowering of Quilts*. Lincoln, Nebraska: University of Nebraska Press, 2001.

Davis, Nancy E. *The Baltimore Album Quilt Tradition*. Baltimore: Maryland Historical Society, 2000.

Goldsborough, Jennifer Faulds, with Barbara Weeks. *Lavish Legacies*. Baltimore: Baltimore Historical Society, 1994.

Havig, Bettina. *Carrie Hall Blocks: Over 800 Historical Patterns from the College of the Spencer Museum of Art, University of Kansas*. Paducah, Kentucky: American Quilter's Society, 1999.

Joyce, Henry. *Art of the Needle: 100 Masterpiece Quilts from the Shelburne Museum*. Lachine, Quebec, Canada: Transcontinental Press, 2003.

Kimball, Jeana. *Red and Green: An Appliqué Tradition*. Bothell, Washington: Martingale / That Patchwork Place, 1990.

Nachmanovitch, Stephen. *Free Play Improvisation in Life and Art*. New York: Tarcher, 1991.

Nelson, Cyril I., and Carter Houck. *The Quilt Engagement Calendar Treasury*. New York: E. P. Dutton, 1982.

Nickels, Sue. *Machine Appliqué: A Sampler of Techniques*. Paducah, Kentucky: American Quilter's Society, 2001.

---. *Machine Quilting: A Primer of Techniques*. Paducah, Kentucky: American Quilter's Society, 2003.

Sienkiewicz, Elly. *Baltimore Album Revival! Historic Quilts in the Making*. Lafayette, California: C&T Publishing, 1994.

---. *Baltimore Elegance*. Lafayette, California: C&T Publishing, 2006.

Wagner, Debra. *Traditional Quilts, Today's Techniques*. Iola, Wisconsin: Krause Publications, 1997.

# Resources

## Aurifil Thread

**Headquarters:**

Via Como 16
20020 Solaro, Milano, Italy
+39 0296799694
Fax +39 0296793175

**USA:**

500 N. Michigan Avenue, Suite 300
Chicago, IL 60611
312-212-3485
Fax 312-276-8028
www.aurifil.com
info@aurifilusa.com
Aurifil has a color card of thread
weights and colors that will make it
easier for you to match threads to
your fabrics.

## Cherrywood Fabrics, Inc.

P.O. Box 486
Brainerd, MN 56401
888-298-0967
www.cherrywoodfabrics.com
Cherrywood sells a color card that
features all the colors of hand-dyes,
including rayons, T-shirts, threads,
and more. It also has cherry rolls
and a grab bag that is perfect for
appliqué when you only need a
smidgeon of something.

## Clover Needlecraft, Inc.

13438 Alondra Boulevard
Cerritos, CA 90703-2315
800-233-1703
www.clover-usa.com
customercare@clover-usa.com

## Cutter Bee Scissors

EK Success
www.eksuccess.com

## Hand Appliqué Method

**Holly Mabutas**

Eat Cake Graphics
www.eatcakegraphics.com
holly@eatcakegraphics.com

## Robert Kaufman Fabrics

Box 59266, Greenmead Station
Los Angeles, CA 90059-0266
310-538-3482
800-877-2066
www.robertkaufman.com
Robert Kaufman has a swatch
card for Kona Cottons that can
be ordered through Hancock's
of Paducah. The website is
www.hancocks-paducah.com.

## Lecien Corporation Art/Hobby Division

**Division Headquarters:**

Yotsubashi Grand Square
1-28-3 Shinmachi
Nishi-ku, Osaka 550-0013 Japan
+81-6-4390-5516
Fax +81-6-4390-5526
www.lecien.co.jp/en/hobby/

**Lecien U.S.A., Inc.:**

5515 Doyle Street, Suite 6
Emeryville, CA 94608
510-596-3085
Fax 510-596-3004
info@lecienusa.com

## Machine Quilters

**Marty Vint**

Dogwood Quilting of Baltimore
www.picturetrail.com/dogwoodqlt
dogwoodquilting@aol.com

**Melodee Wade**

408-985-0446
melodeewade@aol.com

**Shelley Nealon**

www.quiltedbliss.com
shelley@quiltedbliss.com
408-246-1122

## The National Quilt Museum

215 Jefferson Street
P.O. Box 1540
Paducah, KY 42002
270-442-8856
www.quiltmuseum.org

## Northcott Silk, Inc.

**Canadian Head Office:**

640 Rowntree Dairy Road
Woodbridge, ON L4L 5T8
905-850-6675
Fax 905-850-7197

**USA Office:**

1099 Wall Street West
Lyndhurst, NJ 07071
201-672-9600
Fax 201-672-9675
www.northcott.net

## Soft Fuse Fusible Web

Shades Textiles
Marietta, GA 30060-9302
800-783-3933
www.shadestextiles.com

# Index

## Patterns

# About the Author

Annie Smith made her first quilt in 1980 and began teaching in 1984. Teaching a variety of techniques, fabric selection, and machine appliqué are her areas of expertise and what she has become best known for. She began sewing when she was a Brownie Scout, and in high school her entrepreneurial spirit helped her make money with her own sewing business, making clothes for friends and then clients.

Annie's twenty-year career in technical assistance and corporate training helped her hone her teaching skills and improve her quilting classes.

She began designing quilts and patterns during the dotcom bust when her full-time job moved overseas. Her pattern company, SimpleArts, evolved from a family business and successful pattern company into a burgeoning online presence when *Quilting Stash—The First Podcast for Quilters* was created in 2005. Her audience, which has grown exponentially over the years, listens from locations all over the globe in more than one million households. In 2009, Annie added online quilting classes to her Internet offerings, bringing classes and unique quilts to quilters everywhere.

Annie teaches at national and international quilt guilds and was Artist in Residence at the Empty Spools Seminar at Asilomar in 2009 and Elly Sienkiewicz's Appliqué Academy in 2010. She was a featured guest on the second season of Alex Anderson and Ricky Tims's *The Quilt Show*.

Her work has been featured in *Quilters Newsletter*, *McCall's Quilting*, and *Professional Quilter* magazines, and she was a contributing writer for *Quilter's Home* magazine.

Annie's enthusiasm for quilts led to the creation of an extensive local quilt show event, A Bountiful Harvest, which took place in 2002 and 2004.

Annie is a fifth-generation San Josean and Californian. She lives with her family: her husband, Guy, who assists with every aspect of her quilting business, and daughter Kirsten and son Robin, who both know how to make quilts and their own clothes. Annie's middle son, Ryan, and his wife, Karen, live in North Carolina with Annie's first granddaughter, Cambria Rose.

*Annie's website:* www.simplearts.com

*Annie says:*

Although I teach common things, there is nothing common about my approach to quilting and teaching. I am intensely interested in adding value to whatever I undertake, which, I believe, makes what I do definitive. I love to teach and mentor students and encourage them to understand their inherent creativity.

*Annie loves quotes. Her favorite quote is:*

What would you do if you knew you could not fail?
—*Robert H. Schuller*

# Great Titles *from* C&T PUBLISHING

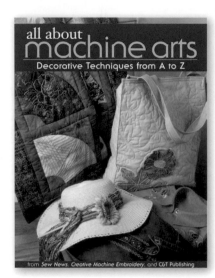

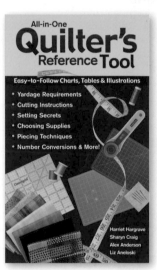

*Available at your local retailer or* **www.ctpub.com** *or* **800-284-1114**

For a list of other fine books from C&T Publishing, ask for a free catalog:

**C&T PUBLISHING, INC.**
P.O. Box 1456
Lafayette, CA 94549 | Email: ctinfo@ctpub.com
800-284-1114 | Website: www.ctpub.com

C&T Publishing's professional photography services are now available to the public. Visit us at www.ctmediaservices.com.

**Tips and Techniques** can be found at www.ctpub.com > Consumer Resources > Quiltmaking Basics: Tips & Techniques for Quiltmaking & More

For quilting supplies:

**COTTON PATCH**
1025 Brown Ave.
Lafayette, CA 94549
Store: 925-284-1177
Mail order: 925-283-7883 | Email: CottonPa@aol.com
| Website: www.quiltusa.com

Note: Fabrics used in the quilts shown may not be currently available, as fabric manufacturers keep most fabrics in print for only a short time.